THE
TRADER
JOE'S
ADVENTURE

TURNING A
UNIQUE APPROACH
TO **BUSINESS** INTO A **RETAIL**
AND **CULTURAL PHENOMENON**

LEN LEWIS

Dearborn™
Trade Publishing
A **Kaplan Professional** Company

President, Dearborn Publishing: Roy Lipner
Vice President and Publisher: Cynthia A. Zigmund
Acquisitions Editor: Michael Cunningham
Senior Project Editor: Trey Thoelcke
Interior Design: Lucy Jenkins
Typesetting: the dotted i

Published by Dearborn Trade Publishing
A Kaplan Professional Company

Printed in the United States of America

05 06 07   10 9 8 7 6 5 4 3 2 1

Library of Congress Cataloging-in-Publication Data

Lewis, Len.
    The Trader Joe's adventure : turning a unique approach to business into a retail and cultural phenomenon / Len Lewis.
        p.   cm.
    Includes bibliographical references and index.
    ISBN 1-4195-0013-9
    1. Trader Joe's (Firm)—History.   2. Grocery trade—United States—History.   3. Supermarkets—United States—History.   4. Chain stores—United States—History.   5. Specialty stores—United States—History.
    I. Title.
    HD9321.9.T73L49 2005
    381′.456413′00973—dc22

                                            2005003632

Dearborn Trade books are available at special quantity discounts to use for sales promotions, employee premiums, or educational purposes. Please call our Special Sales Department to order or for more information at 800-621-9621 ext. 4444, e-mail trade@dearborn.com, or write to Dearborn Trade Publishing, 30 South Wacker Drive, Suite 2500, Chicago, IL 60606-7481.

Contents

Introduction

Over the past 75 years, the supermarket industry has taken more forms and formats than anyone can remember. It evolved from the old neighborhood general store and small public market model—where customer service was in vogue—to one sporting behemoth supercenters the size of several football fields. Now, automated self-service checkouts—the ultimate in impersonal service—are increasingly common.

This same industry became the great equalizer in society, resulting in the democratization of food and other consumer products. Thanks to supermarkets, people of all social classes were privy to a previously unknown freedom of choice—the opportunity to buy fresh foods at fair prices. The early years gave rise to industry icons such as the A&P, Safeway, Publix, Kroger, King Kullen, Piggly Wiggly, Jewel, Albertsons, IGA, and a seemingly unending roster of chain and independent retailers. Each tried to be a little bit different from the other. These markets sprang up in everything from old abandoned garages to urban storefronts and sprawling shopping centers. They became a ubiquitous part of the landscape, dotting suburbia and rural towns across the country, and looking as American as the apple pies they sold in their bakeries.

As time went on, consolidation eliminated differentiation. The need to cut costs and to roll out stores more quickly resulted in a cookie-cutter approach to retailing. Mom-and-pop stores gave up ground to a new generation of megaretailers, most of which look pretty much alike. Yet, through it all, one grocery retailer managed to survive—and flourish—by being different. It's an unlikely contender with a name and operational strategy as offbeat as the products it sells: Trader Joe's.

This relatively small company based in Monrovia, California, has been the subject of considerable discussion—and envy— among consultants, competitors, and other retail industry observers who have tried to dissect and analyze its improbable success. And now, for the first time, this book will do the same, offering insights into how these proven strategies can be applied to virtually all types of businesses.

The success of Trader Joe's is all the more remarkable considering that the supermarket industry in the United States is vastly "overstored." Far larger competitors are fighting tooth and nail for a share of the consumer's heart, mind, and wallet. Most stores have a difficult time differentiating themselves from the competition, and few cater to the increasingly diverse demands of today's shoppers.

When all is said and done, the key for Trader Joe's lies in the simplicity of its operation and clarity of purpose. It lives to offer customers unique, high-quality private label products at a fair price. It accomplishes this goal in somewhat retro, small but comfortable environments, which remind people more of an old-time grocery than a modern supermarket. This laidback style has served Trader Joe's well for decades, and over the past ten years the chain has emerged as one of the savviest niche retailers in the world—on its way to becoming a national (and perhaps someday global) phenomenon.

Since its founding more than 35 years ago, Trader Joe's has not only kept people coming back but has also created its own culture and a cadre of loyal shoppers who aren't the least bit bashful about extolling the store's virtues to perfect strangers. Even more interesting, this diminutive retailer has operated in the shadow of some of the nation's largest and most competitive chains. As you'll discover, they seem to regard Trader Joe's the way an elephant sees a gnat—somewhat annoying but not troublesome enough to waste time and energy trying to swat.

Californians have known about Trader Joe's since the late 1960s, when entrepreneur and wine lover Joe Coulombe dreamed up the concept of a small, unpretentious store with a tropical theme. The idea was meant to combat a new retail concept called 7-Eleven. Coulombe stood out by stocking his convenience store with gourmet foods and budget wines that were largely manufacturer closeouts. Using this strategy, he not only managed to survive the onslaught of 7-Eleven, he flourished in a market starved for budget gourmet foods and was, in many ways, ahead of his time. To this day, Trader Joe's continues to stand out in an industry that talks about differentiation as a key business strategy but rarely achieves it.

Trader Joe's is clearly on the move. Up until a few years ago, the chain consisted of only about 50 stores, most of them cocooned in old California strip malls more reminiscent of 1950s retailing than a radical new style of retailing. But this unique grocery store is now on its way to becoming a national chain. According to some observers, it could grow to 2,000 or more stores over the next decade, taking its quirky brand of fun, funk, and creativity to a much wider and eclectic assortment of customers, including culinary adventurers, health food freaks, microwave aficionados, and anyone looking for high-end foods at relatively low prices.

Customers of Trader Joe's are as unique as the chain itself. They are not shoppers who value convenience, low prices, cigarettes, and six-packs. Instead, Trader Joe's has been called the supermarket for both out-of-work PhD's and those who are over-educated and underpaid. "A dream grocer for yuppie epicures in search of Tasmanian feta cheese and carrot ginger dressing" is how one observer describes the chain. Others see it as a destination for shoppers who are more likely to pack up the family and head for Morocco than Disneyland or for those more interested in Garcia Banquero Iberico cheese than Velveeta.

Although its customer base is not considered upscale by any means, Trader Joe's consumers have relatively high household incomes and a propensity for social activism. Furthermore, their ardor for the company is such that they are not above lobbying local politicians, real estate developers, and the company itself to get a store in their neighborhoods. In fact, loyal customers lacking access to a local Trader Joe's have been known to pack an extra bag for a little shopping trip when they travel to a city where the chain is located. Talk about loyalty!

Fortunately, success has not spoiled Trader Joe's. Its cheesy tropical and nautical décor—right down to the fishnets, plastic lobsters, and Hawaiian shirted "crew"—is still a staple of every store. Its name has become synonymous with creativity, operational excellence, quality products, and a fun shopping experience. The chain is clearly one of the darlings of the industry and the envy of every retail executive from Boise to Berlin, producing sales per square foot upwards of $1,300—more than double the industry average. This gives the typical Trader Joe's store about $12 million a year in sales—in an average of 12,000 square feet. While the privately held chain does not disclose financial results, analysts have estimated annual sales to be in the area of $2.6 billion and climbing.

While such results are usually reserved for retail giants like Wal-Mart, Costco, Target, and Home Depot, Trader Joe's knows that size doesn't matter. Plastic lobsters aside, the chain's success is based on the high level of trust it has built with shoppers since its inception—trust largely based on listening to its customers and providing the high-quality store brands that constitute 80 to 85 percent of its merchandise mix.

But this selection is also dictated by a keen focus on consumer health and environmental concerns. For example, the ahi tuna is caught without nets, peanut butter and hamburger buns are organic, cleaning products are eco-friendly, and even the chocolate raisins are gluten-free.

For these and other reasons, Trader Joe's stores are not just popular; they have achieved cult-like status among a loyal group of customers that includes health food fanatics, gourmets, and chocoholics. When a new store opens, those familiar with the chain often line up well in advance, hoping to be among the first to stroll down the aisles.

This loyalty is also evident among employees. Labor relations in the retail industry are at an ebb—strained to the limit over wage disputes and health benefits—but people line up for jobs at Trader Joe's. *Fortune* magazine has consistently ranked the company among its 100 best places to work. Of course, it doesn't hurt that compensation is generally much higher than the local supermarket competition. Even part-timers start at $8 to $12 an hour. First-year supervisors can earn over $40,000. Store managers, or "captains" as they are called, can pull in upwards of $140,000. And this doesn't even include the additional 15 percent the chain contributes to each employee's retirement fund.

But dollars and cents are only part of the Trader Joe's story. This operation values its employees as much as its customers. Their work is truly appreciated, their opinions matter, and they often determine which of the company's unique products make it to the shelves. In turn, they are friendly and interact with customers to a degree unheard of in most conventional supermarkets.

This curious and unlikely combination of upscale marketing, downscale pricing, old-school retailing, tight cost control, limited selection, almost nonexistent advertising, and lots of fun has been combined with a sense of humor and adventure. Anyone who doubts this should check out the chain's *Fearless Flyer,* a whimsical newsletter that talks about the chain's latest products in a folksy style and sports graphics straight out of a Victorian primer—or a Monty Python comedy sketch. It's actually one of the few bits of advertising the company does, and it's far more successful than some multimillion-dollar campaigns by competitors.

Because Trader Joe's has mastered operational disciplines that elude even the most sophisticated retailers, many retail industry experts say the chain defies any neat description or standard categorization. By all rights, the very things that make it successful should be a recipe for disaster. Its average store is only about half the size of even the smallest neighborhood supermarket these days. Each location only carries about 2,500 items, compared to an average of 25,000 at conventional supermarkets. And instead of large, easy-to-access locations, most are housed in relatively small, older strip shopping centers with limited parking.

Trader Joe's makes the extra effort worth it by catering to those who expect nothing less than a culinary treasure hunt when they come through the front door—instead of the usual drudgery normally associated with grocery shopping. This is accomplished through the efforts of a relatively small group of 18 to 20 buyers, who circle the globe looking for unique products that can be sold exclusively by the chain under its various labels. The company is also constantly innovating, introducing products such as the now legendary Two-Buck Chuck wine, which sells in most stores for $1.99 a bottle and set the entire California wine industry on its ear.

Throughout *The Trader Joe's Adventure,* you'll go behind the scenes of this notoriously tight-lipped company to get a better sense of how it operates. Among other success factors, we'll explore:

- How the company manages to stand out in such a hyper-competitive, commodity-driven industry
- The inside story of Aldi, the huge German-based parent company of Trader Joe's, which is run by the reclusive billionaire Albrecht brothers
- How Trader Joe's became a student of consumer behavior and created a fun and entertaining shopping experience for customers
- Ways the company cuts out intermediaries to keep costs down and maintain control over its products
- How and why it developed a real estate strategy focusing on underdeveloped and less expensive sites
- The real story of how Two-Buck Chuck was created and why this innovative move forever changed the entire wine industry
- Why Trader Joe's employees are so happy and how the company created such an employee-friendly work environment that instills strong loyalty
- Ways the much smaller Trader Joe's outsmarts competition six times its size—over and over again
- Why the company spurns traditional advertising and public relations, instead relying primarily on word of mouth and other unconventional marketing means.

Perhaps Gretchen Gogesch, head of Chicago-based Integrale and a longtime Trader Joe's watcher, put it best when she said, "They [Trader Joe's] are really retail anthropologists. They keep an eye on how people spend their leisure time, what they read, and how they can fit into people's lifestyles. They don't just understand consumer behavior, but the whole consumer—right down to their pets."

It's an operating philosophy that far larger retailers have failed to grasp. And now, for the first time, you'll come to understand how this underdog David is on its way to becoming a Goliath of the retailing world.

CHAPTER 1

Dare to Be Different

If you tuned into Los Angeles classical music station KFAC during the mid-1970s, you likely would have heard an unusual commercial that began something like this: "This is Joe Coulombe with today's words on food and wine." Coulombe wasn't your everyday news commentator. He was promoting the latest food finds for the fledgling grocery chain he'd founded several years earlier, which had come to be known as Trader Joe's.

Granted, it's not exactly your typical screaming radio advertisement. After all, other stores were busily hawking the week's lowest prices for toilet paper, laundry detergent, and ground chuck—not just on the radio but also on television and in weekly circulars. But Coulombe took a far different strategy from the rest of the pack. His ads were more like lectures, taking on such heady questions as "What is Bordeaux?" and "How does this year's vintage compare with last year's?" Unusual for sure. Then again, we're not talking about your average Joe. Coulombe, and the grocery chain he founded, have never done anything even remotely typical.

THINK OUTSIDE THE BOX

The stage was set for what would ultimately become known as Trader Joe's. Back in the late 1950s, Southern California was enjoying a postwar boom and an unprecedented growth in population as people came to the Golden State in search of the California dream. They were also attracted to the allure of a laidback lifestyle in the warm California sunshine. It was about this time that Joe Coulombe, a 1954 graduate of Stanford University's business school, presented an unusual business plan to some of his former professors. He proposed to build gourmet food stores full of items purchased in bulk and then repackaged and sold at moderate prices to well-educated, but not necessarily wealthy, customers. His professors reportedly didn't buy into the idea, which isn't that surprising, considering that true gourmet stores were few and far between in those days. Those stores that did well focused exclusively on high-income shoppers. In addition, at this time national brands were kings. Consumers, whose tastes in food had yet to break out of the ordinary, were more interested in Philadelphia brand cream cheese than trying a French Neufchâtel at any price.

However, like any good entrepreneur, Coulombe was undeterred. He went forward with his plans and purchased the Pronto convenience stores in 1958. Pronto consisted of an unremarkable group of three small outlets in and around the burgeoning Pasadena area. As the influx of immigrants from eastern states continued unabated, food retailing in Southern California was a solid, highly profitable business, without the razor-thin profit margins and labor strife that exist today. The large chains competed with both each other and smaller independent grocers. Pronto focused on specialty items and closeouts. It had little competition and did extremely well servicing a niche that no one else had gone after. But during the socially turbulent 1960s, Pronto faced a threat that could have put Coulombe's fledgling business on the skids. A new outfit called 7-Eleven, which had begun in Texas 30 years earlier, was aggressively moving westward, along with the population. In 1963, 7-Eleven purchased the Speedee Mart chain in California, entered the franchise business, and really began to take off.

Legend has it that Coulombe was vacationing on a beach somewhere in the Caribbean, trying to figure out what to do about this new competition, when he decided to adopt a tropical theme and focus on building no-frills stores with deeply discounted gourmet products. He also took inspiration from the novel *Trader Horn,* which chronicled the travels of a trader and adventurer in Equatorial Africa during the 19th century. It was just the kind of thing that intrigued Coulombe, who had a love of travel and discovery. He finally changed the store's name from Pronto Markets to Trader Joe's in 1967.

While the beach thing may be more urban folklore than fact, Coulombe was unquestionably an astute businessman and a student of human nature. He knew people were most comfortable trying out new experiences and cuisines while on vacation. His idea was to create a fun environment where people with champagne tastes and beer budgets could feel like they were on holiday. He began to double the floor space of his stores and decked them out with cedar plank walls and nautical décor. Meanwhile, employees added to the ambiance by wearing colorful, Hawaiian-style shirts.

Coulombe took the idea of exotic retailing one step further, when he began buying closeouts and overstocks from gourmet food manufacturers. He also purchased bargain wines from overstocked distributors or importers—even from winemakers who were up against the financial wall. This was a risky move in the 1960s and 1970s, as many of the items he stocked were unfamiliar to most consumers. But shoppers responded well to this retail upstart. Trader Joe's offered hard-to-find goods they couldn't get at the local supermarket. Although few closeouts are on the shelves at Trader Joe's these days, this early strategy boosted the chain's reputation for uniqueness and for turning a mundane shopping trip into a treasure hunt. Furthermore, Coulombe's shrewd vision enabled him to eliminate national brands. This meant he wouldn't have to rely on lowball pricing to compete with other stores.

CATER TO YOUR CUSTOMERS

In the early days, Coulombe said he was aiming for the "educated consumer." This was another total departure from a mass-market concept like grocery retailing. Coulombe knew he couldn't get every grocery shopper and didn't want to try. He knew that being all things to all people was not what Trader Joe's was about. A few retailers at the time were targeting a more up-scale clientele, but they were pricey and out of reach for the average shopper. Supermarkets were just discovering the concept of one-stop shopping and the mass retailing mantra of "pile it high and let it fly." It would be another decade or more before most supermarkets even approached the idea of catering to specific demographic groups and even longer before the concept of differentiation came to a head in the industry. Even today, most supermarkets continue to struggle with the concept of differentiation, and few are successful in this quest.

Coulombe was a pioneer in developing the notion that "one size does not fit all" in retailing. From the beginning, Trader Joe's brought the concept of impulse buying to a whole new level. In effect, the entire store was geared toward impulse shopping—or buying what you didn't know you needed. Traditional supermarkets pretty much limited impulse items to end-aisle or register displays—a practice that continues today.

Along with this concept of differentiation came the philosophy that with the right customer base, and conceding that your store will not completely replace the traditional supermarket for the average weekly shopping trip, national brands were not necessary. In fact, carrying them would be detrimental and simply make Trader Joe's look like every other food store.

This differentiation is what attracted German grocery giant Aldi to Trader Joe's, which it ultimately acquired from Coulombe in 1978 after nearly two years of on-again, off-again negotiations. Aldi, known for entering markets quickly and usually under the retail radar, rarely buys other companies. However, it originally entered the United States in 1976 with the purchase of the Benner Tea Company in Illinois, a chain that operated small stores similar to those run by Aldi in Germany. Talks were also held with the Jewel T limited assortment store chain in Chicago that would have enabled Aldi to get a stronger foothold in the lucrative Midwest market with stores similar to its European model. But Jewel T management at the time viewed Aldi as an unfriendly suitor that would have made an unfriendly shareholder. Aldi backed off, not wanting to waste time and money trying to convince them otherwise. Interestingly, Aldi still got its way in 1982 when it acquired a 10 percent interest in Albertsons, based in Boise, Idaho. Albertsons now owns the Jewel-Osco food store chain—Jewel T's successor after years of mergers, acquisitions, and consolidations.

Despite this setback, the Germans really wanted an investment in the Western states. Aware of Aldi's interests, a U.S. investment company operating in Germany investigated Trader Joe's. "I went there to take a look at it and immediately knew what a fine company this was. It was a true specialty store," says Dieter Brandes, a well-known author and consultant who was an Aldi executive for 14 years and a member of the chain's administrative board. During his tenure, Brandes shepherded the acquisition of Trader Joe's. He declined to discuss the price Aldi finally paid for the chain but calls it "an amazing deal."

BE DIFFERENT

When discussing Trader Joe's, Brandes invokes the work on corporate competitiveness by author and business guru Michael Porter, a professor at the Harvard Business School and one of the leading authorities on competitive strategy. "He [Porter] divided companies into three types—the differentiators, the cost-conscious, and all the others that are in between with no specific concept," Brandes observes. "Trader Joe's was clearly a differentiator and so much different than any store in the United States or anywhere else at the time."

The reason for its success was Joe Coulombe, whom Brandes calls one of the most imaginative entrepreneurs he's ever met. Coulombe was intent on developing a new style of retailing by purchasing the best imported products and selling them at reasonable prices. He visited France and Switzerland at least twice a year to buy wine, cheese, and other delicacies. He also honed the store's focus on health foods and, when Aldi came calling, was already deeply invested in private labels.

At the time, Trader Joe's operated 23 stores, all of them reflecting Coulombe's laid-back tropical concept. The most intriguing of the bunch was the Hollywood store, which was lined with walls of autographed pictures from all the movie and television celebrities who regularly shopped there.

After visiting California and striking up a strong personal relationship with Coulombe and his wife, Brandes invited him to Germany for a meeting with Theo Albrecht, who, with his brother Karl, founded Aldi. "I met him at Düsseldorf airport and asked if he wanted to have lunch," says Brandes, who ticked off some of the city's most exclusive restaurants for Coulombe's consideration. "All he wanted was to have some real German wurst."

Coulombe and Albrecht got along fairly well at those early meetings. After all, they were two highly focused, creative entrepreneurs who had built up their businesses from scratch. When

Albrecht first saw Trader Joe's, he knew it was the right move to buy the chain because its corporate culture was similar to Aldi's. Plus, the stores were alike in size and in their limited selection of goods.

Joe Coulombe was not as enamored of Aldi and, at several points, stopped the negotiations. It was not a money issue. Rather, he felt that Trader Joe's and Aldi would be like mixing fire and water. He realized the two companies were much alike in many ways, even though they operated at different ends of the retail spectrum—Aldi focusing on low-income consumers and everyday groceries rather than gourmet items. "But he grew increasingly anxious as the negotiations went on," Brandes shares. "He was concerned about the differences in merchandise assortment. But mostly he saw Aldi as an organizational machine—everything well organized and fixed in place. This was very different behavior than what he was used to."

Coulombe was also concerned about his employees, many of whom had been with him from the start. "At the time, he owned 60 percent of the company, and the employees owned 40 percent," Brandes says. "He felt responsible for his people and was a little afraid of the changes Aldi might make once they took over—including changing the name to Aldi. But that was never our intention." After about nine visits to Los Angeles to meet with Coulombe and his employees, Aldi executives finally closed the deal in 1979.

No immediate changes were made to the operation. But eventually discussions got around to cost control and instituting some of Aldi's operational policies at the California chain. Apparently, these talks did not sit well with Coulombe, and he eventually retired in 1988, when the chain had 26 stores and was doing $145 million in sales. As Brandes puts it, "He [Coulombe] is an entrepreneur—not an employee." Some observers believe that Coulombe's relationship with Albrecht, which became tenuous over the years, simply soured. The two locked horns on every issue from merchandising and store staffing to cost containment. Interestingly, tightfisted cost control has always been one of the cornerstones of Trader Joe's success, along with a cautious store expansion program and limited promotional activity.

Coulombe's talent and creativity did not go to waste after the sale. While he is no longer part of the Trader Joe's operation, at this writing he remains a member of the board of Cost Plus World Markets as well as Bristol Farms—a chain of small upscale supermarkets in California. He continues to travel extensively and posts reviews and comments on food and wine from all over at his Web site, http://www.winejoe.com. He regularly includes treatises sharing his thoughts about wines from around the world.

Interestingly, there seems to be little, if any, crossover between the day-to-day operations of Aldi and Trader Joe's today. "I think Trader Joe's sells more merchandise out of boxes and pallets, which is probably something that came from Aldi. But they still have their own buyers, knowledgeable people who know food and wine and buy directly from vendors in Europe and elsewhere," says Brandes, who feels that Trader Joe's must be taking advantage of Aldi's considerable resources and buying clout to some degree.

MAKE BIG MOVES IN SMALL STEPS

Although Coulombe was an entrepreneur, and Trader Joe's was clearly his brainchild, he was not above asking people he respected for advice. One was John Shields, a college acquaintance who would later become the company's CEO. Shields says that Coulombe began fooling around with the initial concept for Trader Joe's while the stores were still operating under the Pronto banner. "I helped Joe write the original business plan, what we called at the time the 'white paper,'" Shields said several years ago in a rare interview with professor Mark Mallinger at Pepperdine University. "Over the years, he would send me the monthly reports and a whole series of things. So, I really followed the company very closely and added some of my own ideas. Trader Joe's has just been an evolution."

Shields's most challenging task when he ultimately became CEO in 1989 was determining whether or not to expand the business. Even now, at more than 200 stores, this discussion continues to rage among industry pundits. However, discussions are now centered not on whether the chain should expand, but rather on where and how quickly Trader Joe's can grow without losing sight of the factors that have made it so successful.

Shields recalls that, in 1991, he was concerned about the company's long-term growth. He believed the West Coast could perhaps support 100 stores but was concerned about prospects for the geographic expansion of such a quirky company. "We had the Pacific Ocean on the west, Canada in the north, Mexico in the south, and desert and mountains in the East," he recalls. "Realistically, there weren't any population centers until you got to the Midwest. That meant making a geographical leap to the East."

Interestingly enough, Aldi never intended to take Trader Joe's national. The only strategy in the beginning was to move north toward San Francisco. "It wasn't common at Aldi to make long-term strategic plans," Brandes observes. "The company liked going step-by-step. Coulombe was the same way. There was no specific formula. He just improved things step-by-step. [It was] a slow evolution."

The problem was that few retailers of any stripe had been successful in making a big geographic leap. What made Shields even more nervous was his experience with the Mervyn's department store chain. Mervyn's tried this same strategy and stumbled badly in going from the West Coast to Texas.

Not wanting to make the same mistake twice, Shields and his team took a full year to put together a business plan for expanding Trader Joe's. The target became the 500-mile corridor from Boston to Washington, D.C., which had more colleges and universities than any other area in the United States. They dubbed it "Trader Joe's country."

This approach to expansion was considered conservative. Even so, Shields estimated that the stores would lose money for the first three years, possibly approaching the break-even point by the end of that period. The decision was made easier by the fact that Trader Joe's had turned into a cash cow on the West Coast and was able to finance its expansion internally. Even without stockholders or Wall Street analysts looking over its shoulder, this company hates debt and paces growth by profitability. Every new store is paid for out of the cash flow that the chain generates. Borrowing capital to accelerate growth is a no-no. "As long as you don't have competitive pressure to maintain market share, there's no reason to accelerate store rollouts or go outside for capital," says Alex Lintner, a senior analyst with The Boston Consulting Group.

Trader Joe's, as well as Aldi, continue to follow this strategy religiously. It's the primary reason store growth has been slow but steady, unlike growth at many companies in the retail food industry that end up burdened with a debt-heavy balance sheet brought about by overexpansion. Furthermore, no one is trying to copy the Trader Joe's concept in a major way, so the company has no reason to hurry.

Early on, there was a question about whether Trader Joe's eclectic offerings would translate 3,000 miles from its West Coast enclave. "We spent a lot of time on this issue and finally decided we could do it by moving about 25 existing employees to the East Coast," Shields says.

The first two Trader Joe's stores on the other side of the country opened in Boston in 1996. Just three years later, another 25 locations had opened in the Boston to Washington corridor, all of which were breaking even. By 2001, the region was home to 48 highly profitable stores. The chain's network, encompassing more than 215 stores, now covers 18 states, including Arizona, California, Connecticut, Delaware, Illinois, Indiana, Maryland,

Massachusetts, Michigan, Nevada, New Jersey, New Mexico, New York, Ohio, Oregon, Pennsylvania, Virginia, and Washington.

At present, Trader Joe's continues its aggressive expansion in the Chicago area and surrounding markets in Illinois, Michigan, Indiana, and Ohio. It also plans to open as many as ten stores around Minneapolis/St. Paul, Minnesota. However, one of the most interesting developments, and one which several observers say is long overdue, is its move into New York City with multiple locations ranging from 9,000 to 12,000 square feet. This will pose some potential challenges to the company. First, although real estate in the Big Apple is readily available, it doesn't come at the bargain rates Trader Joe's gets in its usual out-of-date and often empty suburban strip malls. It will also have to compete with the plethora of small gourmet shops that dot every neighborhood.

Still, as electric as Manhattan may be, Trader Joe's offers a shopping experience arguably different from anything the city has ever seen—namely gourmet foods at discount prices. When it does open stores in New York City, sales are expected to be phenomenal, surpassing those in any of the chain's other stores. Even Trader Joe's executives may be surprised by the outcome.

New York is virgin territory and a perfect market to target the chain's core customers—the overeducated and underpaid. In New York City, residential real estate prices are in the stratosphere, and it's not uncommon for people to pay $2,000 a month or more for one-room studio apartments. This means that a significant percentage of their earnings goes toward rent, leaving only a small discretionary income—particularly among the area's younger residents. For them, Trader Joe's represents an affordable indulgence.

Whole Foods, which has been described as the nearest thing to Trader Joe's in terms of gourmet, healthful foods and extensive private labels, is also taking on Manhattan. Its stores in the downtown Chelsea neighborhood and uptown in the massive Time Warner Center have become destinations for residents and visitors alike. But the Trader Joe's concept is more distinctive. In Manhattan, as in other markets, it will teach people to shop differently and demonstrate that the terms *gourmet* and *bargain* are not mutually exclusive.

The brilliance of the simple, yet remarkable, concept is that it can comfortably coexist with other retailers. This is a boon to concentrated urban areas like New York City, where the chain operates shoulder-to-shoulder with grocery stores, bagel shops, and an unending string of takeout cuisines. The stores are small enough to attract New Yorkers who don't like spending more time than they must on shopping for food. But they also present an eclectic selection of items that people won't find anywhere else, and certainly not at such discounted prices. In fact, a typical Trader Joe's store does $12 million a year in sales. Units in a busy urban center like New York City—without a parking lot—could produce twice that amount, according to some observers. But this growth won't come without its challenges.

The inner city has been called the final frontier of American retailing. It's been ignored for decades by retailers and developers, who instead made a beeline for the open space of the suburbs or rural-like exurbs.[1] Inner-city retailing is a completely different animal. Construction is expensive and delays—whether caused by contractors, unions, or city inspectors—are all too common. Real estate costs in these areas will be astronomical compared with what Trader Joe's now pays and could easily top $30 per square foot. The customer base will be far more diverse in terms of ethnicity, income, and education. Deliveries are also a constant headache because of inner-city traffic patterns. Then, there's the issue of loss prevention and other security matters, which Trader Joe's existing stores don't deal with on the same scale. Clearly, the chain faces challenges. But if history is a guide, it will successfully meet them all head-on.

LOOK AHEAD

Invariably, any discussion about Trader Joe's turns to the question of exactly how big this little chain can get. With stores currently in only 18 of 48 contiguous states, there's clearly a lot of room for expansion. But this is never going to be an Anyplace, USA, concept. It is somewhat limited by demographics, though not as much as some might think. In successfully becoming bicoastal, Trader Joe's proved it was more than just a quirky little company catering to Southern California's freaks and health nuts. It is a transferable concept and one of the few successful stories in the world of retailing.

Depending on whom you talk to, Trader Joe's could end up being a 1,000-store to 2,000-store chain. With its own capital base and Aldi's considerable resources lurking in the background, there's virtually no limit to where the company can go or how quickly. Trader Joe's has always financed its own expansion, and this strategy is likely to continue. Moreover, Aldi's involvement is probably unnecessary given the type of inexpensive, secondary real estate locations Trader Joe's prefers. Without question, the company is big on recycling dead space.

Trader Joe's probably could become a truly national chain. But the difference between Trader Joe's and others that have made such a move is that the company is in no hurry and no one is pushing it. "There's no wind at their back," according to Ken Harris, a partner in the consulting firm of Cannondale Associates. "The only thing that's pushing them is a following across the country and pent-up consumer demand. But there's no bottom-line need to be national the way there is at a company like Kroger."

As many retailers know, the problem with growth is not a matter of real estate but in maintaining a consistent corporate culture and not abandoning what made them successful in the first place. As Kevin Kelley, a principal in the design and consulting firm of Shook Kelley notes, "The number one enemy of any organization is growth—and growth that takes place too quickly. This is an organization that's about innovation, not operational efficiencies. When organizations grow, they bring in managers to help solve distribution or human resources problems. Sometimes these people can strip-mine the strategy out of the organization."

However, Trader Joe's has been very smart about growth, and there are no signs the strategy is deteriorating. The company takes its business model and cross-indexes it with marketing areas that skew high according to characteristics it looks for in its customers. The bottom line is that Trader Joe's can pretty much pick the area in which it wants to grow. But the company is likely to be well aware of what growth rate it can sustain before going over the edge.

There's also the issue of evangelizing more people to retain the culture that's been built—not an easy task, considering that every retailer in the nation is struggling with people issues: finding, training, and retaining good employees. Trader Joe's has a generous employment package, which we'll discuss in depth in Chapter 9. More important is the attitude of your team. Former CEO John Shields has always credited having a clear vision and communicating it to the entire organization as one of the reasons for the company's many accomplishments—both then and now. In Shields's time, part of this involved spending at least two days a week visiting stores and listening to employees and customers. This practice continues today under the leadership of current CEO Dan Bane. Bane says he, too, likes to visit stores, work the registers, talk to customers, and wear a nameplate with the title Chief Cart Runner. "It goes back to hiring the best people you can and giving them the tools they need to do the job," Shields says. "I have always encouraged people to be entrepreneurs. I guess the last thing I'm famous for saying is 'have fun.' I used to go to all of the prestore openings and talk with all the new people for about two hours. I always ended up saying, 'At the end of 30 days, if you're not having fun, please quit.' They'd look at me with these big eyes. You spend most of your life at your job. If you're not having fun, get out of here."

That same philosophy has also been applied on the consumer side. The décor is meant to convey an informal, freewheeling, feel-good environment, where shopping is an adventure and you never know what you might find around the next corner. It's kind of like Disneyland for foodies. While this represents a big difference between Trader Joe's and other retailers, the casual atmosphere is no accident. This company has a well-organized, carefully analyzed business plan. It just so happens it also has a cult following.

In the supermarket industry, one thing that is usually well planned—always far in advance—is advertising and promotions. Since its inception, the supermarket industry has touted weekly specials through an expensive combination of weekly ad inserts, full-page run of press ads, radio, television, and direct mail. Many chains are now going high-tech to promote special buys. Stores are using technology like in-store kiosks, television screens in the aisles, terminals attached to shopping carts, online coupons, cell phones, and other wireless devices that enable shoppers to get the specials on their car radios before reaching the store. Behind all the high-tech gadgetry and reams of newsprint, super-market advertising hasn't really evolved beyond price-oriented promotional vehicles, most of which look pretty much alike. One reason is that everyone is carrying almost identical items and getting the same deals from national brand manufacturers.

Trader Joe's has a carefully planned advertising and promo-tional vehicle, which also hasn't changed much since first being created by Coulombe, unlike anything used by the competition. Radio ads still feature down-home commentary delivered by company executives. Meanwhile, the *Fearless Flyer* is a monthly company brochure and marketing piece printed on inexpensive newsprint paper and filled with clip art that looks like it was lifted from a Victorian-era magazine. Madison Avenue ad executives might shudder at the sight of this amateurish-looking brochure. But customers, who pick it up at the store, sign up for it online, or get it in the mail, read it religiously and might easily fly into a rage if it ever changed. There is little chance of that happening. First of all, the chain doesn't have enough stores in any one area to make a major media buy cost-effective. Second, it doesn't carry the national brands that would support a big budget or multimedia campaign. That's why advertising with a low-cost structure like the *Fearless Flyer* is an essential part of the chain's advantaged economic model. Third, changing this format simply wouldn't be Trader Joe's. The chain is less concerned about using advertising to sell products than it is desirous of informing people and creating a need.

What's more, the *Fearless Flyer* is more effective than other mediums because it doesn't just sell products. It gives customers the story behind these items in a lively tongue-in-cheek way that mixes in a few bad jokes, puns, and sometimes a history or science lesson.

The spring 1985 edition is a perfect example. This was before someone came up with the name *Fearless Flyer* and it was simply called *Trendy Foods at Trader Joe's,* but people familiar with the company would recognize the style and tone.

One ad was for "sushi-sized" bottles of Kirin beer for 89 cents. It began with the following lesson: "Japan's beer industry was started by Americans in 1869. The Japanese then turned to Germany for technical advice and the rapid expansion of brewing followed."

Then there was the promotion for Taittinger Brut Champagne at $12.99: "Many of the battles of the first World War were fought in the Champagne region 75 miles northeast of Paris. A young, rich cavalry officer named Pierre Taittinger discovered Champagne while fighting there and stayed on to start his own company."

An ad for jumbo fancy Georgia peanuts at $1.29 a pound gave readers an education on agriculture and politics while promoting the company's prowess as a buyer:

For years the government has had a peanut support program under which it buys peanuts from growers . . . This year, growers have been selling most of their peanuts to the government. The result has been a decrease in the quantity of peanuts in the marketplace and a sharp increase in price. Once again, Trader Joe's was in the right place at the right time, and we were able to secure an offer with a leading peanut roaster.

Fast-forward to summer 2004. The products may have changed, but the style is remarkably similar. Under the headline "Grilli Grilli Yummi Yummi" is an ad for mahimahi fillets: "Sometimes known as dolphin-fish, mahimahi *(coryphaena hippurus)* are actually not related to dolphins. Mahimahi's Spanish name is *dorado* (Spanish translation: golden) because this fish sports a golden color."

Another ad waxes poetic over arugula: "Arugula has been enjoyed by the Italians and the French for centuries. It's become more common in the last 20 years or so when Americans turned from their iceberg lettuce devotion to a mix of greens."

The idea of being different in everything from store design and product selection to advertising strategy has become a trademark of Trader Joe's, a company that has always been ahead of its time. This kind of thinking is more important now than ever. Being different is no longer an option for retailers—it is a matter of survival.

AMR Research, a leading industry consulting firm, talks about "profitable differentiation" in retailing as "blending an atomic-level understanding of consumer demand with effective retail execution to create a profitable and superior shopping experience."

A slightly less scientific definition comes from the great French designer Coco Chanel, who dominated the fashion industry for 60 years. She might have been talking about Trader Joe's when she said, "In order to be irreplaceable, one must always be different."

GO YOUR OWN WAY

Since being launched by Joe Coulombe nearly four decades ago, Trader Joe's has pretty much defied standard definitions of what a retailer should be and how it should act. By making up its own rules, the company has clearly differentiated itself from the rest of the retail pack. It is nowhere near being a supermarket based on accepted definitions of size and selection. And what's on the shelves of this highly successful niche retailer can hardly be referred to as mere *commodities* in any sense of the word—unless raspberry salsa, salmon patties, and natural blueberry waffles are your idea of commodities.

Differentiation within the supermarket industry is something everyone talks about, yet few have achieved it. Doing something differently than the competition is the key to prospering in any business, because it creates a unique identity that attracts consumers and keeps them coming back. It's particularly important in the food business, where all stores look alike and carry pretty much the same items. As a result, customer loyalty is virtually obsolete, and patrons instead look around primarily for the best price.

How can retailers differentiate themselves in such a crowded arena? By creating a reason for shoppers to come to the store! Target has done it with glitzy ads and the "cheap chic" of designer apparel and home fashions. Wal-Mart accomplished it with stores that carry everything—including the kitchen sink—and offer the perception of having the lowest prices around. Krispy Kreme did it with a unique product that became a cult classic but then made the mistake of offering it in every supermarket, convenience store, and railroad station. Kmart didn't do anything unique and slipped into bankruptcy. Despite a recent financial resurgence, the chain is still doing little to create its own footprint in the marketplace.

By examining the Trader Joe's business model, we can identify a number of strategies that can be highly effective when it comes to standing out in the retail industry.

- Offer reasonable prices on a line of distinctive products that can't be purchased anywhere else, thereby creating a bond with customers.
- Have more products that are ready-to-make rather than ready-to-eat to attract those who want to be involved with their food.
- Take a hard look at existing products and don't be afraid to drop those that customers don't need. (They don't need 20 varieties of the same toothpaste or 10 sizes of the same laundry detergent.)
- Hire, train, and retain people who enjoy interacting with customers and are capable of suggestive selling.
- Develop relationships with suppliers based on the research and development of new products not on promotional allowances.
- Know your customers. Find out about their lifestyles and how you fit in—not the other way around. Ask them what they like and don't like and how you can make things better.
- Build stores of a manageable size with a specialty focus.
- Pursue innovation. Don't just copy what the competition is doing.

How does Trader Joe's define itself? A former vice president of operations for the chain put it this way: "It's a mix of supermarket, grocery store, and international gourmet shop with wholesale club pricing." Industry analysts and various other retail experts generally classify Trader Joe's as a specialty retailer or niche marketer. But which niche? Basically, the chain's simple but brilliant marketing strategy is to take a little from each concept and offer great products at fantastic prices. There really are no complex marketing strategies—just good solid execution based on giving consumers something different.

Trader Joe's is simply different from the rest of the food retailing herd, and it stands out in an industry that has long survived on conformity in everything from store design to product selection. By contrast, Trader Joe's is a convenience store with an attitude that matches its outspoken, unique customer base— a group that runs from hippie to yuppie. Over the years, it has made gourmet foods available to a large but not necessarily up-scale audience and single-handedly sent the California wine industry into a tailspin.

The stores may be a bit bigger than in the beginning, but they still remain small by most standards, with the average location running 6,000 to 12,000 square feet. That's one-sixth the size of the average supermarket. Overall selection is narrow, and 80 to 85 percent of the store's 2,000 items consist of Trader Joe's various private labels. (The typical supermarket, by comparison, carries about 25,000 items.) The stores are often erected in vacant spots within old strip centers where the rent's cheap and the amenities are few, making them seem better suited to dollar or closeout stores than a purveyor of gourmet foods.

By being different, Trader Joe's has built itself into a business with estimated annual sales of $2.6 billion, or $1,300 per square foot, which is about twice the supermarket industry average.

The past decade has been an active one for Trader Joe's, with a tenfold growth in profits and a fivefold increase in the number of stores. This growth was a big change from prior decades, when store growth was slower and the chain avoided the over-expansion that has plagued the rest of the supermarket industry. This is perhaps one reason Trader Joe's has been able to fly under the retail radar, more or less coexisting peacefully with larger, mainstream supermarket chains.

On another front, a virtually unseen threat to the supermarket industry is the slow and steady expansion of Trader Joe's parent company, Aldi, which intends to open as many as 40 stores annually in the United States over the next seven to ten years. This move could help to finance a more aggressive expansion plan by its gem of a subsidiary, Trader Joe's. And one thing's for sure: Aldi has shown it is definitely a force to be reckoned with.

CHAPTER 2

Maintain a Consistent Philosophy

In the secretive and often surreal world of the superrich, four of the wealthiest people on the planet are Microsoft chairman Bill Gates, investment guru Warren Buffett, and Karl and Theo Albrecht. While Gates and Buffett are household names around the globe, few have any idea who the Albrecht brothers are, even though they are collectively worth $41.1 billion dollars, according to *Forbes*. Being anonymous is exactly the way they like it. What's more, the Aldi grocery chain they founded over a half-century ago, which is now 6,000 stores strong, is just as much of a puzzle.

While this book is about Trader Joe's and the company's successful business practices, the tale would not be complete without the story of Aldi. Up until several years ago, few—including some in the food business—were aware that Aldi even owns Trader Joe's. Top management at the California-based chain never mentions the German parent company and the relationship between the two. While that relationship is believed to be somewhat symbiotic in nature, it's pretty invisible to outsiders.

Conversely, Aldi, which issues very few press releases on its own operations to begin with, never talks about its ownership of Trader Joe's. Some observers believe this arm's-length relationship is for the best, because the two are very different in terms of merchandising and product selection. However, their operating philosophies are similar in many ways, and we'll explore them in this chapter.

OPERATE UNDER THE RADAR

Even in the ultra hush-hush world of European industry, Aldi is an enigma wrapped in a riddle. It is the third largest corporate entity in Europe, yet its close-to-the-vest attitude makes the CIA look like an open house. Its guarded approach to business seems to have rubbed off on Trader Joe's, also famous for shunning the limelight.

Although new regulations in Germany since 2000 have forced Aldi (short for Albrecht Discount) to be more open about its finances, relatively little is known about the inner workings of the chain. Even those who follow Aldi in Europe are not sure who is running individual operations at any given time. Making things more opaque for outsiders is the division within the company that took place during the 1960s. The company was split into two completely separate businesses: Aldi Nord (North) and Aldi Sud (South). Since then, they've divvied up the world between them, and there is little evidence the two sides come together on anything. Aldi Sud owns Trader Joe's.

Even less is known about the reclusive Albrecht brothers, whose combined fortune through a complicated series of family foundations and trusts was structured to avoid disputes among potential heirs.

In fact, the last time the brothers hit the headlines was in 1971 after Theo Albrecht was kidnapped. This is yet another reason the entire family is so media shy. Apparently, kidnappers looked at this somewhat shabbily dressed man and kept asking him if he was really Theo Albrecht. They then demanded to see his identification after throwing him in the getaway car. After being held for a harrowing 17 days, Albrecht negotiated his own release, rumor has it, getting the kidnappers to drop their price to about 7 million deutsche marks, or a little over $3 million at the time.

When he was released, Theo Albrecht told the German press, "I am healthy, but of course I am very tired. The experience took a lot out of me." That was the last public comment made by either Theo or Karl Albrecht. However, both brothers continued to go about business as usual, expanding their empire across Europe into the United Kingdom, the United States, and, most recently, Australia, where the chain is changing the dynamics of discount retailing.

Several years later, Theo got into hot water with the German government when he tried to write off material damages of the kidnapping from his income taxes. Since then, not even major newspapers like Frankfurt's *Allgemeine Zeitung* have a picture in their archives of this reclusive billionaire that is less than 30 years old.

Moreover, neither the press nor industry experts are completely sure to what extent Theo and Karl are still involved in the business or when—and if—the torch was completely passed to the next generation.

Karl is about 84 (the founders' exact birthdays are never discussed, either) and believed to have retired from day-to-day operations in 1993, leaving nonfamily members in charge of operations in the south. He raises orchids and is said to be a passionate golf fan who still plays regularly on his own 27-hole course. The location of his estate is, of course, unknown. In the north, Theo supposedly lives in a small, one-family house in a suburb of Essen. He still keeps up with the business and comes to work from time to time. However, his two sons, Theo, Jr. and Berthold, are both directors of the company and run the business.

While the personalities that founded this unique privately held chain are a mystery, nothing is vague about Aldi's power around the globe, a power that prompted *Business Week* to run an article about Aldi under the headline "The Next Wal-Mart?". In fact, it may be the only chain on the planet to "out Wal-Mart Wal-Mart" by beating the Arkansas-based retailer at its own pricing game in Germany.

BE NONDESCRIPT

Aldi stores don't exactly look like contenders to win market share in their own backyard, let alone achieve world domination. The stores are small, less than pristine, lacking in amenities, short on staff, long on checkout lines, and limited in selection to one or two brands in each category. Again, the operation is similar to Trader Joe's in many ways.

This "hard discounter" has changed the dynamics of retailing across Europe and is giving fits to competitors in every market from Stuttgart to Sydney. The basis of this success is extreme cost control in every aspect of Aldi's operations, savings that not only go into the company's coffers but also into the pockets of ultraloyal customers from every socioeconomic strata. People no longer view shopping at Aldi as a social stigma or the stores as grubby, low-rent outlets for inexpensive food. Rather, they are seen as champions of the people. In Germany, Wal-Mart tried to be cheaper. But as one observer put it, "No one believed them. People trust Aldi to give them the best price for the best quality."

To understand Aldi and the impact its philosophy has no doubt had on Trader Joe's, one must go back to its Germanic roots. The chain began as a small food shop opened by the Albrechts' mother in the working-class town of Essen before World War II. Their father, a former miner, hired himself out as a baker in a local bread factory. The brothers were working in the family food store when World War II broke out. Theo

Albrecht was shipped off to a supply unit in North Africa while his brother, Karl, was sent to the Eastern front.

After the war, the Ruhr valley, like most of Germany, was devastated physically and economically. War-weary residents of bombed-out neighborhoods had little income and could only afford to buy essential items. But the brothers saw the vast potential for retailing. They took over the family business and soon began acquiring other stores as Germany's postwar economy improved and homemakers clamored for new, inexpensive goods.

From the beginning, the company's guiding principal was to offer a limited number of items at extremely low prices in barebones stores that are virtually indistinguishable from one another—whether located in Germany, the Netherlands, Australia, or the United States.

In fact, this cookie-cutter approach was probably responsible for making Aldi one of the few European retailers to develop a broad network of stores across three continents. Moreover, this pioneer in the discount format has veered very little from its original market positioning. And no matter which market it enters, Aldi usually forces other chains to adapt to its discount format— rather than Aldi changing itself to suit market conditions.[1]

Interestingly, while the world is busy trying to put Aldi into a box, the company itself has never really defined its corporate culture, other than with the one basic operating tenet that gets written into the company's job descriptions: "The way to keep ahead of competition is through the extreme application of the principle of economy."[2]

Dieter Brandes, a consultant and former Aldi executive in Germany, boils the company's strategy down to this—*Konsequent und Einfach*—or consistent and simple. This is also the title of one of his books, in which Brandes identifies the values that form the basis of the chain's corporate culture. Among them:

- *Asceticism.* Stores are simple and spartan with the selection limited to basic products. The stores lack amenities for either customers or staff. Furthermore, the company only provides basic company cars and economy-class business trips.

- *Simplicity.* This extends to structure, store format, product range, technology logistics, and marketing.
- *Economy and extreme cost awareness.* Continual efforts are made to avoid unnecessary costs at all levels, from saving paper and electricity to optimizing the use of vehicles.
- *Leadership.* People must conform to the company's philosophy. It looks for employees who are modest, discreet, and self-disciplined.
- *Secrecy.* The company allows no employees to talk to the media and avoids scandal at all costs.
- *Fairness.* Aldi believes in treating its staff and suppliers well, while motivating them to be their best.
- *Focus.* The company adheres to a "customer is king" philosophy.
- *Trustworthiness and predictability.* The chain has gained a reputation for offering the best quality at the lowest possible price.

LOW COSTS, HIGH QUALITY

The dual philosophy of hard discounting and high quality has led to some unprecedented deals with brand-name suppliers. At one time, the company even got Kellogg's to supply corn flakes and other cereals under the Aldi label. However, the Battle Creek, Michigan, company, an icon in the American food industry, backed out after getting flack from other accounts who were unable to compete with Aldi.

Although the spartan atmosphere of the stores kept some people away, extreme low pricing was an immediate hit. This almost religious adherence to the discount format has given Aldi a near cult-like following among fervent bargain hunters. To be sure, the deep-discount approach is an attraction for low-income shoppers around the world. However, as noted, Aldi, particularly in parts of Germany, attracts high-income shoppers who simply know a value when they see one. This demographic is evident when looking in the parking lots of some stores and seeing BMWs and Mercedes, their well-heeled owners waiting in long checkout lines.

Customers didn't seem to mind the limited selection or the small, crowded stores. The Albrechts, on the other hand, relished it, believing then, as the company does to this day, that consumers are looking for value and quality, not for a store to have every product on the market and all the operational bells and whistles. Of course, it also didn't hurt that the limited selection kept inventory, operating, and distribution costs to a bare minimum.

Without question, 1960 was a watershed year for Aldi. Barely a decade old, the company already had some 600 limited-assortment, deep-discount stores in operation. Then the brothers split the operation. As previously mentioned, Aldi Nord was headed up by Theo Albrecht with brother Karl in charge of Aldi Sud. The two entities have the German stores split between them. However, Aldi Nord, run by Theo Albrecht, Jr., controls stores in Spain, the Netherlands, Luxembourg, France, Denmark, and Belgium. Aldi Sud, said to be the more aggressive in some respects, is run by managing director Peter Ernst and oversees the stores in Ireland, the United Kingdom, Austria, Australia, and the United States—including Trader Joe's.

Throughout the years, expansion continued in Germany. But a maturing home market convinced the brothers to look abroad—first in Belgium (where the Aldi stores were called Lansa) and then to the Netherlands under the Combi banner. Aldi came to the United States in 1976, just three years before purchasing Trader Joe's. The mid-1970s were a period of hard times and high inflation, and Aldi flourished in that environment. The chain built its first distribution center in the Chicago area and located stores in lower–middle class towns—poor areas where people would respond to rock bottom pricing, but not where there was hard-core unemployment.

After the fall of the Berlin Wall in 1989, Theo moved into the former German Democratic Republic, where he opened some 400 stores. It was about the same time that Karl moved to the United Kingdom and Ireland with 230 stores in England, 20 in Wales, 17 in Scotland, and 10 in Ireland. The British seemed to have begrudgingly adopted Aldi, though being seen there is still something akin to social suicide, according to Oliver Heins of Planet Retail, a London-based consulting firm. Well-heeled Brits have not adopted Aldi in the same way as their German counterparts. They still don't want to be seen shopping in a store for low-income people. Several years ago, Aldi South began opening stores in Australia, where its discount price structure gave fits to long-established retailers.

Despite an aggressive worldwide expansion program, Germany is still Aldi's most important market, accounting for an estimated two-thirds of its business. But when it goes into a new market, it does so with a vengeance and an intention to stay. In Australia, for example, the company applied to the Australian government for visas to be made available to core management from Germany. And while Australia is a hotly competitive food market, reports in the news at the time indicated that Aldi was ready to fund up to ten years of operational losses.

CHANGING YOUR IMAGE

It is interesting to note that the company's global expansion seems to coincide with the company's new image. Outside the United Kingdom, it is no longer viewed as the poor people's grocer, and it's not a social stigma to be seen carrying an Aldi shopping bag. Now it's the place to be seen, attracting people of all socioeconomic backgrounds.[3] More than 80 percent of the

German population shops at Aldi and, as an article in *NAMNEWS* (an online newsletter for marketing executives) observed: "Cheap is beautiful, stinginess is cool, and Aldi is cult." In fact, low-income consumers only make up about 20 percent of Aldi's customer base. Aldi has become hip, a place for treasure-hunting consumers where chauffeur-driven limousines vie for space with more pedestrian vehicles.

To take advantage of this new image, the chain has published a series of adult and children's cookbooks under the name AldiDente, which are devoted to recipes that only use items available at Aldi stores. These books, including a guide to Aldi's inexpensive wines, have sold more than a million copies. More recently, cookbooks have been supplemented by special brochures, containing menus for special occasions like Christmas and New Year's. Of course, all the items, including champagne, can be purchased at Aldi.

Aldi would probably prefer being viewed as the small, grubby underbelly of the food industry that competitors thought it to be, flying under the competitive radar and snatching away market share before a competitor knew what hit it. But sometimes you just can't go home again. In researching the company and consumer behavior, sociologists have concluded that Aldi has become synonymous with liberty, equality, and brotherliness.[4]

In essence, the chain has morphed into the Robin Hood of the food industry, responsible for the democratization of discount shopping into a socially acceptable activity for everyone, regardless of income or station in life. It is interesting that Trader Joe's has similarly democratized the gourmet food industry in the United States. In essence, the chain has, in its own way, made it okay for customers in all social strata not to pay a lot for gourmet food products that might be prohibitively expensive elsewhere.

LESS IS MORE

For Aldi, the "less is more" philosophy has also made the entire shopping experience less stressful for people. In fact, by standardizing their small stores, Aldi has created a homier, more relaxed shopping environment than that of gigantic conventional supermarkets, according to sociologists. Although the Aldi limited-assortment store concept was developed for outlets of about 10,700 square feet, most stores are much smaller. In Germany, the average selling area is 7,800 square feet, and in France 7,100 square feet.[5] These are less than one-fourth the size of the average conventional supermarket in the United States. In general, stores in Aldi's southern division are somewhat larger because they are generally newer. The chain's older stores are usually located in the Northern division. But there, too, the company is building new units in both inner-city and suburban locations. Now, as then, there seems to be an overwhelming aversion to debt, and expansion is financed largely from cash flow. The company has clearly instilled these virtues on Trader Joe's, which adheres to the same philosophy. Then again, shared values may have brought these two together in the first place.

The deep-discount, limited-selection format has been the subject of some speculation among Aldi watchers and other retail pundits, some of whom feel that the chain's unwavering devotion to hard discounting was a case of tunnel vision—too narrow a focus considering the ever-changing nature of the supermarket industry in Europe and elsewhere. However, it's hard to argue with success, especially with a company that has been named one of the most respected corporate brands in Europe.

This same operational frugality that places a limit on store sizes and item selection was evident early in Aldi's development. One story has it that when the brothers started carrying butter— still a rare commodity after the war—they didn't want to invest large sums in refrigerated display cases. So employees had to carry the product to the cellar every evening to keep it cool.

Aldi-inspired rumors of cost control and frugality are the stuff of legend. Aldi stores lacked mirrors in the bathrooms, so that employees would spend less time in there. Additionally, the company invested a lot of money in expensive floor covers that looked particularly cheap to maintain a frugal image with customers. Years ago, Theo Albrecht is said to have chastised a manager for ordering four ballpoint pens at one time, asking him to demonstrate how a person could write with all four at once. At one time, Aldi stores had no telephones because Theo Albrecht thought they were an unnecessary expense.

The stores' limited selection seems to be an outgrowth of this operational frugality. The Albrechts knew that carrying few items would lower their operating costs, savings that could then be passed on to customers. In fact, the stores have been likened to the retail environment in East Berlin in the mid-1970s before the Wall and Communism crumbled, with stores carrying just two brands of toilet paper, one brand of pickles, and even a trench coat for $21.[6] There might be 3 kinds of bread but not the 15 or 20 varieties found in conventional supermarkets.

And there's no fancy shelving. Most everything is still piled on pallets or in cut-case cardboard boxes.[7] To keep labor costs down, suppliers are required to deliver goods in uniform crates and pallets. Not surprisingly, shoppers are not immune. For one thing, they have been required to leave a deposit on carts. The money is returned along with the cart, but it helps the store to reduce labor costs. Stores also charge for shopping bags, and only recently have Aldi Nord and Aldi Sud begun accepting debit cards. Aldi was the last German retailer to have a cash-only policy.

Although Aldi Nord and Sud do take advantage of central buying on certain products and seem to be of one mind when it comes to cost savings, these remain completely separate operations that don't share business practices. Both have been broadening the product mix over the past couple of years but at a different pace. For example, Aldi Nord has increased the number of lines it carries to 800 from 600, and Aldi Sud has increased to over 650 lines from about 450. This expansion has made room for more middle-market products as well as nonfood lines.[8] Yet there remains a significant difference in the product mix between the North and South. For example, Aldi Nord stocks baby food while Aldi Sud does not. Aldi Nord has cigarettes while Aldi Sud continues to shun this profitable but theft-prone category. Legend has it that the cigarette issue is what led to the split in operations.

Additionally, when the Northern operation tests new products, it does so across its entire network. It then decides whether a product is successful enough to stay on the shelves. The Southern operation, which oversees about 1,500 stores, is said to be the more successful of the two in terms of offering more competitive prices as well as in introducing new product lines. It does vigorous testing in one or two stores and then slowly rolls it out to other locations. The company did this last year with fresh mincemeat, which turned out to be one of the most successful new product introductions.

Aldi Sud has also been testing freshly baked bread and rolls—a move that mirrors the trend toward fresh foods throughout German retailing but a surprise for a chain that adheres so fervently to basic foods. As with mincemeat and other items, baked goods are being carefully tested in a handful of stores before being rolled out across the entire network, according to Oliver Heins, an analyst with Planet Retail in London.

However, years of conditioning and consistently delivering on a value proposition in every product and category it introduces have given Aldi a real luster. Customers are convinced that by shopping at Aldi, they won't be cheated in terms of price, quality, or value.

This brand identity is backed by a 100 percent satisfaction or money-back guarantee. If customers don't like a product, they simply return it and get their money back. There are no arguments, excuses, or nonsense like vouchers or store credits—

just cash back for something that fails to live up to customer expectations.

TEST CAREFULLY

Unusually early in the process lengthy testing procedures virtually guarantee customer satisfaction. When a product is accepted by regional buyers, it is usually tested in about four Aldi outlets for a period of six to eight weeks, and sales are evaluated on a points system. If a product receives a passing grade, it is given a trial in about 50 outlets.

If a minimum passing grade is obtained in this trial, the product is then eligible to be taken on by all Aldi stores. However, this depends on whether price and supply negotiations with vendors are successful. The entire process, from initial presentation of the product to stocking in stores, may take as much as one year. The extensive testing procedures are understandable given that each store only carries 600 to 700 products—and about 90 percent of them are private labels marketed under a secondary brand name. And many of those secondary brands are produced by national brand manufacturers who can no longer deny the power of the deep discounters in markets like Germany. Private labels are typically priced at least one-third below the leading national brands, and the company uses more than 15 different private labels in its Aldi Nord and Aldi Sud divisions, but different ones in each. The only ones common to both are Albrecht-Kaffee and Tandil, a laundry detergent.[9]

Aldi's protracted testing procedures would be anathema to U.S. supermarket suppliers, which are constantly rolling out new products and use slotting fees and other promotional activity to get these goods on the shelves. However, Aldi is also testing whether suppliers can meet its strict quality standards and fulfill long-term supply requirements. Suppliers really only have to meet four basic requirements:

1. Meet Aldi's price demands.
2. Meet criteria for quality that are very close to those for branded products.
3. Match Aldi's distribution requirements.
4. Stick to a strict delivery schedule.

The process is envied by many in retailing but successfully copied by few. It is meant to establish long-term relationships between the chain and its suppliers, many of which laud Aldi as a straightforward operator that may be demanding but is relatively easy to deal with.[10] As close a relationship as this may be, Aldi does prefer to keep vendors at arm's length to preserve the integrity of its operations. As such, Aldi buying managers are not even allowed to accept dinner invitations from suppliers.

Extensive testing could become more difficult as the company expands its offerings into such items as meats, organic dairy products, and other fresh foods—and as it steps back from its canned-only image.

At most supermarkets, products that don't sell are usually placed on sale or are part of some promotional activity designed to push them out the door. At Aldi, if a certain number of consumers deem a product to be less than satisfactory, it's immediately taken off the shelves, and manufacturers are called to haul it away at their own expense.

Although vendors line up to partner with Aldi and many German vendors wouldn't exist without them, product failures are a source of tremendous humiliation. As one businessman was quoted as saying: "Being called in to Aldi is worse than confessing an extramarital affair to your wife."[11]

But this is all part of the level of trust that Aldi has built up with generations of shoppers—all of it without advertising. Once a week, newspapers publish a nondescript sheet showing the latest items and special offers. Marketers shudder at such a barebones approach. However, people have responded to it for 50 years. When Aldi advertises something really hot, people start lining up for it in the wee hours of the morning, knowing that when it's gone, it's gone.

Such was the case in 2002 when Aldi started selling computers. The item—and there was only one—sold for about 4,400 at the time. It was so popular that Aldi sold about 60 percent of all computers in Germany that year and was single-handedly responsible for the mass computerization of German homes. These kinds of promotions on nonfood items like computers, printers, and even bicycles are being done more frequently. Often tens of thousands of a single product sell out within days, nearly killing the market for everyone else.[12] More recently, stores began doing these types of special promotions for food, something that was considered anathema to Aldi's everyday low-price (EDLP) image.

Aldi is trying to have the same powerful presence in other high volume categories. Over the past several years, the company has expanded its presence in frozen foods to a point where the chain is said to account for 20 percent of frozen food sales in German supermarkets. It is also said to be making inroads in meat, dairy, and over-the-counter remedies. This expansion has led the company to extend opening hours—no small task in a place like Germany where retail opening and closing hours are strictly enforced by the government and, until recently, you couldn't even get a container of milk past 6:00 PM.

However, for most Aldi shoppers, price is the main attraction—everyday low prices that are the same no matter where you are. The company manages to maintain this strategy by avoiding slotting fees for new products and all the co-op and promotional funds available to retailers from manufacturers. Interestingly, it has also kept costs down in stores by installing scanners. Once considered almost anti-technology, Aldi, faced with long lines and the questionable ability of clerks to memorize every price in the store, installed scanners to speed up checkout lines.

Front-end scanners, a common sight in supermarkets since the 1970s, enable clerks to ring up some 70 items per minute compared with 20 items in stores without scanning.

Labor costs and productivity are a key measure of Aldi's success. In most of the company's marketing areas, it shoots for labor costs of no more than 2 percent of sales, even though the company prefers to hire extremely efficient staff than invest in new technology. Some observers believe this cost can be as high as 4 percent in the United States, but this is still a bargain, considering that labor costs at conventional supermarkets account for 10 to 11 percent of sales. This difference alone is enough to make Aldi far more competitive than traditional supermarkets. Factors such as very basic store layout, lack of in-store storage, and the minimal number of products enable the company to operate stores with a very lean staff.[13]

In fact, management is lean throughout the organization. Top management makes all the strategic decisions, which are then implemented locally by operations managers. The company has sales managers who are in charge of about 50 stores each and, under them, regional managers who are usually responsible for 7 to 10 outlets.

Add to this a buying clout that may even exceed Wal-Mart's and the ability to drive costs out of the supply chain, and what you have is a chain that, like Trader Joe's, has been virtually invulnerable to competition.

CHAPTER 3

Cut Out the Middleman

*"Never tell people how to do things. Tell them what to do,
and they will surprise you with their ingenuity."*
—GENERAL GEORGE S. PATTON

O n first blush, you wouldn't think the late military leader's
philosophy would have anything to do with retailing—
particularly with a rather informal, unmilitaristic environment like Trader Joe's. By some accounts, Patton wasn't exactly
a people person of the warm, fuzzy, and trusting variety. But he
was aggressive in battle, had the respect of his troops and his offi-
cers, and certainly didn't have any trouble getting his point across
to friends and foes alike.

The mark of a true leader—be it in the military, business, or
politics—is based on effective communication and the ability to
know when to dangle a carrot or stick in front of people. When-
ever possible, it's preferable to use the former, because you want
people to follow you for the right reasons. This kind of leadership and management style is more art than science. In the long
run, skilled retail practitioners will be successful by gaining the
loyalty of employees, customers, and vendors alike.

Cutthroat competition in the supermarket industry has created razor-thin profit margins, where pennies sometimes make
the difference between red and black ink. As a result, retailers,

wholesalers, and manufacturers who spent much of the last decade or so throwing around terms like *partnering, collaborative planning, efficient consumer response,* and *efficient assortment* often find themselves in adversarial positions, with each side spending more time telling the other what they *can't* do rather than exploring new possibilities.

Trader Joe's has always been the proverbial horse of a different color. Evoking General Patton's comments about people and ingenuity, the chain's buying and procurement practices are fairly unusual in the supermarket industry. Its relationships with suppliers in the United States and abroad have been true partnerships rather than adversarial relationships. Trader Joe's gives manufacturers detailed specifications, along with the price it's willing to pay, then leaves vendors to their own devices in creating high-quality, unique items. This is much the same strategy as used by its parent company, Aldi.

COUNT YOUR PENNIES

In today's retail environment, it's typical to hear suppliers complaining about customers squeezing them for every penny. Making money and keeping costs down is the name of the game. It would be financially irresponsible for any company to operate in any other fashion. But when it comes to Trader Joe's and Aldi, there is no game playing or abuse of power. For these chains, the overriding philosophy seems to be akin to the biblical expression: "Do unto others as you would have them do unto you." In dealing with suppliers, this means fair, equitable, and respectful treatment. The company's attitude was summed up by one bakery producer who said, "I always thought we were good at what we do. But they actually made us better."

This chain knows the capabilities of its vendors, the demands of its customers, and the dynamics of the marketplace. It also has a clear idea of where its stores fit into the picture. To quote

Theodore Hesburgh, former president of the University of Notre Dame, "The very essence of leadership is that you have to have a vision. It's got to be a vision you articulate clearly and forcefully on every occasion."

For Trader Joe's, this vision means cutting out the middleman and buying direct from suppliers everywhere from Texas to Thailand. This strategy, which takes an enormous amount of marketing, advertising, and supply chain cost out of the system, enables the chain to hold down retail prices on a wide range of specialty and gourmet items that traditionally have carried premium price tags. In effect, this pricing strategy has contributed to the democratization of gourmet foods by making them more readily available to customers at all income levels.

CREATE PROPRIETARY BRANDS

A big part of this vision includes developing brand recognition. The vehicle for this is an extensive, high-quality, eclectic, and very profitable private label program that is probably one of the most successful in the United States—on a par with Sainsbury and Tesco in the United Kingdom when it comes to quality. It has become the chain's main weapon in efforts to build customer loyalty and differentiate itself from competitors—even far larger ones with their own private label programs.

Private label has always been a part of supermarket retailing in the United States. A century ago, A&P was one of the nation's premier purveyors, to a point where its Eight O'Clock coffee became the best-selling brand in the country. Later, the fictitious Ann Page was as much a household name as Betty Crocker. Private label was pushed to the background in the late 1940s and 1950s when national brands, using both radio and the relatively new medium of television, burst onto the scene. The national brands then started paying hefty fees for shelf positions and became even more attractive to retailers. To counter this, private labels tried to position themselves as low-priced brand knockoffs, even copying the packaging. But they only succeeded in becoming second-class, lower-quality products with inferior graphics—and they usually got the worst shelf positions.

More recently, grocers began pushing private labels to boost their own profitability and to build the stores themselves into a brand in efforts to win back both upscale shoppers and bargain buyers who were flocking to alternative formats. This strategy gave rise to a consumercentric approach in everything from product development to sales and marketing. It has also raised debate on what constitutes a balanced retail portfolio with an optimal assortment of national brands and private label products.

Meanwhile, private labels have been outperforming national brands in many categories. Research by ACNielsen indicates that 75 percent of supermarket categories now have a private label presence, and private brands are the sales share leaders in about 25 percent of the categories.

On average, 20 to 25 percent of products sold in supermarkets are private label. This is a respectable number, and it is certainly growing. In Europe, private labels account for 35 to 45 percent of sales, paced by Germany—Aldi's home base—the United Kingdom, and Belgium. Adding to the trend is the "premiumization" of private labels on high-quality items ranging from health and beauty care to pet food. Research by the IGD Europanel revealed that 90 percent of consumers felt that private labels and branded goods were equivalent in terms of quality. Many of their responses were based on experiences at Aldi.

MAKE IT YOUR OWN

The true power of private labels is evident at Trader Joe's, where 80 to 85 percent of nonalcohol products are represented by store brands under such whimsical monikers as Trader José for Mexican items, Trader Giotto for Italian goods, and Trader

Ming for Chinese fare. While many items can be found on a regular basis, the mix changes all the time, because the stores are small and space is at a premium. Moreover, an estimated 20 to 25 new items are introduced weekly. By constantly bringing new products into the mix, the chain has developed a following among customers who much prefer strolling the aisles, looking for interesting and exotic items like frozen French onion soup, than trudging through conventional stores for the usual national brands.

In conventional supermarkets, private label products basically fall into two categories: premium and value products (both of which can bring in new users and create customer loyalty). Similarly, Trader Joe's does not see private label products as one homogenous group and breaks down total store offerings into three tiers.

1. *In-and-out products that only show up once or hit the shelves at certain times of the year and disappear after they've sold out.* This is planned obsolescence and may account for 15 to 20 percent of the company's offerings. It fosters a treasure hunt mentality and keeps customers coming back. These items alone are enough to generate considerable repeat business.

2. *Everyday products like pastas, salt-free marinara sauce, and other staples that are in stock all the time but not always from the same supplier or in the same packaging.* Still, these are items consumers will likely not easily find anywhere else.

3. *A limited selection of branded products, particularly in the wine and beer sections and candy sections.* Many of these are from regional or local manufacturers and are considered quasiprivate labels in that they are exclusive to Trader Joe's. These can account for 20 to 40 percent of the assortment.

Traditional grocery stores take on "new" items all the time to draw customers' attention. But most of them are "me too" items or line extensions of existing products. Trader Joe's uses a few featured items to give people a reason to come back week after week. Moreover, a healthy balance of other brands adds to the legitimacy of the store rather than cannibalizing sales of the company's own products.

To a degree, Trader Joe's also segments the product mix by market. There are core products like marinara sauce and peanut butter dog biscuits that go across all stores. But they are also willing to spice up selection—and sales—in different markets depending on consumer tastes. This gives the organization's buyers enormous leeway to develop products for individual geographic areas.

DEVELOP CAREFULLY

Product development is a touch-and-go proposition. If you're not careful with product development, you can cater to customer whimsy and end up flushing a lot of money down the drain trying to sell jalapeño cat treats. Trader Joe's is certainly smarter than that. But the chain lives in what's been described as "the world of why not." "If someone says to them you can't offer a wine at $2 a bottle, they say, 'Why not?' and go out to find someone to develop it," says Ken Harris, partner and consultant with Cannondale Associates in Chicago. Simply put, there's a constant foraging for new ideas, and the chain prides itself on being ahead of the curve on new trends in niche products.

"We developed a process of aggressive buying that takes out the middleman," says Trader Joe's CEO, Dan Bane. "We'll never have Coke. We decide what we want to place in customers' mouths."[1] More than that, the private label strategy has shaped the consumer's buying experience and tapped into cultural trends far more quickly than conventional supermarkets. It doesn't hurt the top and bottom lines, either, because sales and profits are kept in-house.

SATISFY YOUR SUPPLIERS

Suppliers are enamored of Trader Joe's because, like Aldi, it does not demand the slotting fees, promotional allowances, rebates, or discounts that push costs back on manufacturers. This is a powerful platform from which to negotiate with suppliers, and the chain's buying power is enough to drive prices down. Beyond that, payments are often made in cash and—partly due to the resources of its parent company—are always on time. What's more, delivery schedules are predictable and unauthorized deductions on invoices, a common practice between manufacturers and conventional supermarket chains, simply don't happen.

The company also offers suppliers volume guarantees against price guarantees. Basically, if you create an item exclusively for Trader Joe's that is very different from anything else on the market, and therefore something the competition can't easily do a price comparison on, the chain will sign a multiyear deal to carry it. If you ask suppliers, many will tell you that Trader Joe's is their most efficient and profitable customer. Moreover, once you hit the company's specs and meet its price expectations, executives won't be "in your shorts" all the time. They trust suppliers to do what they were contracted to do, enabling the chain to run a lean and more profitable organization.

In some ways, Trader Joe's operates on the same principles as Wal-Mart but without the hard-line buying strategy that squeezes every last penny out of vendors. They want what they want and pay fairly and regularly. "They don't cause vendors anywhere near the headaches of a regular supermarket," says Alex Lintner of The Boston Consulting Group in San Francisco. "They don't want slotting or promotional allowances, just the best price. And if you deliver it, they'll make sure they sell it."

SEEK HIGH-PROFIT MARGINS

Store brands not only enable Trader Joe's to differentiate it-self from other retailers but are also far more lucrative than na-tional brands. The latter simply would make the chain more vulnerable by locking it into a low price strategy that wouldn't suit the operation or its customers. In fact, Trader Joe's starts out with a significant advantage and can squeeze an immediate profit margin of 15 to 20 percent on products that would only yield pennies for national brands. Margins may be far higher than that on many items because of the high-end positioning. But it is also because Trader Joe's carries a limited variety—not the profit-draining 25,000 to 30,000 items found in conventional supermarkets.

For example, rather than carrying five sizes of a product from three different manufacturers, Trader Joe's concentrates on the fastest-selling items from one or two suppliers that can be han-dled efficiently. This efficient procurement gives the company a significant price advantage. It has reduced the cost of handling simply by reducing the item count. This all translates into a more efficient retail operation. It parallels the strategy that is so suc-cessful at Aldi and produces a return on sales that is believed to be far higher than other chains.

Still, efficiency does not replace innovation. Take the com-pany's corn chowder, which is packaged in a can that is thin on the top and bottom and thick in the middle—kind of a reverse hourglass. A traditional grocery buyer—and manufacturer—might give you all the reasons they couldn't do this, saying it would be difficult to ship and hard to stock. However, these com-panies are driven by operational efficiencies, not innovation, which is really the driving force behind Trader Joe's. Similarly, years ago when M&M Mars came out with Combos, Trader Joe's decided it wanted to get into the pretzel business. They could have worked with Mars on a private label product but chose a different route. They went to other suppliers, who came up with a pocket pretzel filled with peanut butter, now one of the chain's most successful snack items.

Moreover, private labels have created a level of trust between Trader Joe's and its customers that is not enjoyed by most retailers. The products may be supplied by manufacturers all over the world, but they are given legitimacy when the Trader Joe's name goes on the label. It has become a tacit seal of approval, something that, in the past, was limited to only a few of the most revered national brands.

When it comes to private labeling, Trader Joe's and Aldi are on the same page—just different parts of it, with Trader Joe's catering to lovers of value-priced gourmet fare and Aldi targeting the low-income consumer—at least in the United States. Even that may be changing. Aldi had always differed from its discount competition by offering high-quality "economy" basics under names like Beaumont coffee, Kirkwood chicken, Nanny's baby products, and Clarissa and Reeva household items. But Aldi, whose stores are 95 percent private label, broke the mold in 2004 by introducing an exclusive line of over 50 gourmet products under the Grandessa label, including such items as roast chicken and portobello mushroom ravioli, sun-dried tomato salad dressing, artichoke garlic salsa, and cherry ice cream. Also in the lineup is fire-roasted vegetable pizza with artichokes for $2.49, marinated artichoke quarters at $1.99, and a 13-ounce box of mango chai granola cereal for $1.99.

Is Aldi using the new label to move its merchandise mix closer to that of Trader Joe's? Perhaps. Grandessa clearly indicates that Aldi is trying to slowly shed its image as a chain strictly for low-income shoppers. It's an interesting development, because Aldi carries far fewer items than Trader Joe's—600 to 700 versus 2,000 to 2,500. However, with more than 700 stores over 26 states, Aldi is three times as large.

BUY CAREFULLY

The Trader Joe's buying group, while extensive in scope, is fairly small for an operation of this type. From 15 to 20 buyers are constantly traveling. They have thousands of vendor relationships and are visiting hundreds of suppliers and potential new ones annually in search of the latest delicacy—be it Tasmanian feta cheese or morello cherries from Eastern Europe. About 25 percent of the chain's suppliers are overseas. This is an exhausting prospect. Take Doug Rauch, president of the chain's East Coast operations. He was a buyer for Trader Joe's from 1977, about the time the chain began expanding its private label program, to 1994. In his last year, he flew to 16 countries including Thailand, India, Singapore, Hungary, and the Czech Republic. "Sourcing is a lot like prospecting. It's luck and knowledge," he says.[2]

In the case of Trader Joe's, knowledge is a definite advantage because the company has relationships with thousands of vendors and, at any given time, is dealing with hundreds of them—about 25 percent overseas. This is certainly a complex way to do business. But, as the chain's own Web site points out: "We act as purchasing agents for our customers."

Those in the industry certainly agree with this assessment. The Trader Joe's way differs from traditional supermarkets, which have garnered a reputation for merely restocking shelves. "Grocery companies don't buy," says Neil Stern of McMillan/Doolittle Consultants. "Suppliers come to them. They negotiate, then write orders and reorder. But they don't actively buy. Along comes Trader Joe's, and they are out in the market seeking out supply partners with something different. They are not looking for slotting fees, advertising allowances, or General Mills to stop by with the latest selection of products."

Stern continues, "They are out there scouring the market for unique items. If they can get popcorn from some obscure place or licorice from Australia and get exclusive rights to it, that's what they are going to do." On the more mundane side, they are constantly looking for private label suppliers in specialty niches like vegetarian, healthy, ethnic, and even "decadent" items utilizing fresh ingredients.

Whether Trader Joe's is leveraging Aldi's global buying power seems to be a matter of opinion. Some feel the parent company must be involved somewhere along the line—at the very least with new suppliers in Europe. However, most believe there is little, if any, overlap in buying functions. The two chains have far different suppliers and supply philosophies. "Trader Joe's was very successful without Aldi years ago, and now they don't need Aldi to make things happen," says Harris. However, the entire buying process may become increasingly challenging as Trader Joe's expands. As purchase quantities increase, maintaining quality—particularly in refrigerated products—will become more difficult.

MIX UP THE MIX

At present, Trader Joe's is constantly replacing existing items or variations—tweaking the mix. Finding the right product mix "is an ongoing process," says Pat St. John, the director of marketing for Trader Joe's. The company introduces 20 to 25 products a week, and "Sometimes we're right, and sometimes we're not," she says. "If we're not, we don't order it again, and we let it run out . . . Sometimes, that makes some customers unhappy."[3] This is another characteristic that makes Trader Joe's work—its relationship to success and failure. A product that doesn't make it with consumers is not a failure but is seen as a great learning experience for the organization.

Killing an item and quickly moving on to something else would be a far more difficult strategy with national brands due to long-term promotional deals, ad allowances, and slotting fees. But as the Trader Joe's concept matured, product continuity became necessary, and about 80 percent of what's on the shelf is now pretty stable in terms of availability.

In reality, the buying process is only the first step in getting a product on the shelves. Whether Trader Joe's goes to specific suppliers or suppliers come to the chain with exclusive new items—which is increasingly the case—the item has to meet rigorous specifications and testing before it's approved for a spot in the store.

Suppliers know that Trader Joe's has the most rigid standards in the industry. In fact, some vendors who deal with Whole Foods Market can't get their products into Trader Joe's. Peanut butter–filled pretzels is the type of product people drive 15 miles to get. If Trader Joe's starts putting out items that taste like a similar and readily available Frito Lay mass-produced food, it runs the risk of losing all the credibility that's been built up over time. The need for distinctive products means the company has some very tough specifications. For instance, if a supplier is developing an Oriental product for Trader Ming, the chain specifies the exact size of the noodles, how they want the item to taste, and the size of the package. "They know that no supermarket will have a competing product," Lintner says. "This allows them to have a price that seems attractive to consumers while maintaining a healthy margin. It's all based on good competitive landscaping."

Additionally, in dealing with manufacturers, Trader Joe's likes to spread out the business. Generally, supermarkets strike a deal with a manufacturer to put half of the company's product portfolio on the shelves. But Trader Joe's doesn't want one bakery company supplying 40 different items. In some cases, it prefers to have 40 bakeries supplying one item each. The company picks the vendor with the best coffee cake or bread, and that's who supplies that category. Those vendors can vary considerably on a market-by-market basis, sources say.

When it comes to choosing new items, the determining factor is not who has the best deal but rather how it tastes. Some organizations would assign a committee or task force headed by a senior vice president to be in charge of the testing function. Instead of having one person look for trends and new items, Trader Joe's has made that part of everyone's job—from administrative support to senior vice presidents. When it comes to coming up with ideas for new items, the prevailing attitude is that there are no bad ideas.

TEST, TEST, TEST

At present, the company reportedly maintains informal testing panels on each coast consisting of shoppers, store employees, and managers, as well as people from its buying and marketing departments. Manufacturers are not allowed to attend. Sometimes these tastings can be held twice a day, three or four days a week. These sampling sessions not only include the company's own products but also other brands. "This is not an insular organization that incestuously looks at its own products," says retail industry consultant Gretchen Gogesch. "It has a healthy respect for others and very wisely looks outside the organization to see who is doing great work and what the latest consumer hotspots are. That's when they ask how they can marry that to create their own winners." Aldi, likewise, is sampling private label items every day as well as conducting laboratory tests and making comparisons of its own items against leading brands.

At times, separate tastings are held for store employees to familiarize themselves with the product so they can answer questions from customers. Employees are also authorized to open up any product that customers want to taste and are encouraged to be honest with people about which products they like and which ones they don't. In turn, customers can often be the best salespeople for Trader Joe's through word of mouth. It's clear from talking to customers that they rarely are let down by the quality of a new product—be it crackers or corn chowder.

Trader Joe's uses the typical Aldi discipline of putting a product initially into perhaps 15 stores to see how it goes. If sales are big enough, the test is broadened. If that works, it's put in all stores. Velocity and sales per square foot are key measures. As previously noted, the company's sales per square foot are about twice the industry average. But the chain will also hold onto products without the expected velocity if the product is an image builder for the company.

KEEP A WATCHFUL EYE

Once products hit the shelves, they are under constant scrutiny. Trader Joe's employs no elaborate category management system. Tracking the performance of products is sometimes as simple as e-mail notes from store managers to buyers and other members of the executive staff about what's selling and what's not. In effect, the final arbiter of what Trader Joe's sells is its customers. In a perfect world, this is the way it would be. However, in the conventional supermarket industry, what customers want is often secondary to how lucrative the latest deal is from the manufacturer.

This may change if the grocery trade continues to consolidate. Fewer players mean even greater pressure to keep prices down on national brands. Private label sales have been growing faster than brands across most categories for the past three to five years, and there's no reason to believe that won't continue. This makes store brands a unique opportunity to increase the bottom line.

It's not that Trader Joe's is against deals. Since its inception, and because of the limited number of items it carries, the chain has done an outstanding job of procuring leftover inventory from manufacturers. It was very astute at finding manufacturers and either buying a section of a product run or taking the last 50 cases of something at a discount. In the beginning, Trader Joe's was basically in the closeout business, and private labels were nothing more than thinly disguised surplus items. This changed as the company grew and manufacturers started coming to them. Today, little, if any, items in Trader Joe's stores are closeouts.

Not that closeouts or surplus goods denote poor quality. Anything less than top-quality merchandise is simply unacceptable to the store's buyers, and this is the way it's always been. Even though it sources are worldwide, the company maintains quality control standards that are typically above the national brands, according to industry observers. However, it also avoids some of the problems inherent in conventional supermarkets by staying away from categories that could give it trouble.

This means limiting exposure to highly perishable products like meat and produce. These categories do not play a big role at Trader Joe's because they are not categories customers really come to the store to buy. Even as it grows, the chain is not likely to deviate from its current path. As one retail industry observer noted: "Customers aren't upset about not having a big selection of these items, so why should Trader Joe's be? History tells us that private label is what makes them successful. They make it work, and that's where they should stay."

The company has been extremely successful in specialty frozen foods—particularly ethnic items. However, Trader Joe's only has a few facilities that distribute most of its products to stores, cutting down on supply chain problems. By primarily using third-party warehousing and distribution, the company has been able to take the cost out of the system and keep prices down.

By most accounts, the chain's relationship with its suppliers is more than the usual supply-and-demand scenario. It's a genuine partnership in the sense that the chain works very closely with the suppliers it chooses. Often, Trader Joe's initiates ideas with suppliers. A case in point is Joe-Joe's, a hugely successful Oreo cookie knockoff.

Even discussions with suppliers are done on a different plane than with many chains. "I spent time with a couple of their buyers. They are very respectful and collaborative, even in conversations with prospective suppliers," notes Gogesch. "There's none of the braggadocio that some buyers have coming to the table. If you had to characterize them, I would call them polite and dignified—and they operate with a lot of integrity." Some hold the opinion that these characteristics may have rubbed off from Aldi. While this may be a vast generalization, observers firmly believe that European companies have a greater respect and sensibility for the things that got them to where they are. In the case of retail, that's a combination of appreciation for customers, employees, and suppliers.

However, just because a product gets on the shelf, and relations with suppliers are cordial, doesn't mean the product's going to stay there. This cooperative relationship is also very strict when it comes to maintaining quality, another trait of Aldi. "A friend of mine runs a bakery in Germany near Aachen, and one of the items they make is stollen," notes Cannondale's Harris. "They sell the product to both Trader Joe's and Aldi. Aldi inspectors go into their plants at least ten times a year, and they have even more exacting specs than the bakery on what is acceptable quality."

Because Trader Joe's and Aldi have such similar values, no discussion of procurement and buying would be complete without discussing the parent company separately. Despite the intensely competitive nature of the European market—particularly in Germany—taking it out on suppliers through intimidation and abuse of power is simply not the Aldi way of doing business.

Of course, suppliers are dismissed from time to time. This is the nature of the retail business. But dismissal is always for cause and that cause is usually related to poor quality goods. Other than that, Aldi's dealings with vendors are based on "best practices" that are among the strictest in the international business community.

In addition to being able to set your watch by the way the chain pays suppliers, bribes or even the most innocent gifts of any kind are *verboten*. "There is no such thing as a free gift," according to Dieter Brandes, a former Aldi executive and Germany-based consultant. "Any supplier who genuinely wanted to show their appreciation would remember the sales assistants, not just the purchasing agent. This is not an easy rule, because one central purchasing agent at Aldi can be responsible for negotiating annual volumes of anywhere from 1 to 2.5 billion Euros."[4] Even invitations to lunches and dinners are rejected. Apparently, the biggest gift that can be accepted is a calendar.

When it comes to reordering or replenishment, Aldi and Trader Joe's—due to minimal space and items—have a similar philosophy in that they avoid complex inventory control systems. Aldi in particular operates on a simple Japanese inventory control principle known as *kanban*. This literally means "replace whatever is gone." For many items, store managers only order a week's supply.[5]

Moreover Aldi is unyielding when it comes to price. Ken Harris notes:

> Some suppliers would say, "We'll make it to your specs, but we have to charge more." This is not an option. It's a matter of tough love. You have to figure out a way to hit their specs and not raise the price. You have a target you have to hit, whether it means increasing production efficiencies or getting a better deal on raw ingredients. They even suggest ways you can improve your operation. But at some point, you have to hit the line. They don't do it to be obstinate. You just have to take the medicine if you want to do business with them.

CHAPTER 4

Make It Fun

F ew would put the words *fun* and *grocery shopping* in the same sentence. After all, for most people, a trip to the supermarket is little more than one of life's inconvenient necessities. It's an activity you find a way to make time for, not one you actually look forward to. But from the very start, Joe Coulombe longed to create an experience for shoppers that would be much different. He wanted to make a routine trip to the store enjoyable. This philosophy continues to be central to the operations of Trader Joe's today.

This doesn't exactly stand out for casual observers. From the get-go, it's an inconvenient place to shop. The parking lots are small and crowded, and you usually have to fight for a spot with others who are just popping into the local bagel shop, card store, or dry cleaners located in the same shopping center. The inside of the store is just as cramped. This is especially true on weekends, when negotiating the chain's diminutive red shopping carts up and down the narrow aisles is like steering bumper cars at the local amusement park.

Then there are the checkouts—so few that the lines can be excruciatingly long during peak times. There you are, trying to figure out where a line ends as it snakes around the organic bread aisle and halfway down to the area with all-natural soft drinks. To make matters worse, many of the customers in line are still shopping, picking up that package of English muffins that catches their eye, or going back for the yogurt smoothie or mango lemonade drink they like so much but forgot to throw in the cart. Others are just ambling along slowly as they read the latest *Fearless Flyer,* catching up on new items with Trader Joe's own brand of folksy humor.

But there's a reason these lines are so long. Trader Joe's has created an event out of going to the store. It has taken a bland, boring, repetitive chore and created an adventure that begins when you walk through the door. You'll immediately hear the sounds of rock-and-roll music playing in the background. Clerks are dressed as if they are on a summer vacation, with shorts and shirts with a tropical motif being the usual uniform. Then there are the cheesy plastic lobsters, fishnets, life preservers, and a con-glomeration of other low-cost decorations adorning the worn wood-paneled walls. In remodeled stores, murals and paintings of local scenes have replaced some of this nautical whimsy, but each location still sports basically the same décor it offered 15 years ago.

In the back, a tropical-style hut, replete with a thatched roof that looks like it was lifted from a 1950s B-movie set, is used as a sampling station. This area is usually crowded with a steady stream of people trying to make a meal out of the latest peach salsa, mango lemonade, couscous, or macaroon sample that a cheerful and chatty store associate is offering. And, more often than not, by the time they finish tasting the product, customers are heading to the shelf to buy what they've just sampled.

This personal touch doesn't require the technology so preva-lent in today's supermarkets. Until recently, Trader Joe's didn't even have electronic scanners, a requisite part of any normal supermarket's operation these days. For years, the company felt scanners were too impersonal and didn't believe that the technology was in keeping with the chain's down-home, old-fashioned image. Truth is, scanning was also viewed as an expensive capital outlay—a fiscal sin for a company with the reputation of running one of the tightest financial ships in the industry.

DON'T BE ALL THINGS TO ALL PEOPLE

Granted, not all of this sounds like the stuff from which memorable shopping experiences and long-term loyalties are made. In fact, many of these shortcomings would no doubt drive some customers into the arms of the nearest big-box supermarket, which is more likely to have wide aisles and sky-high displays of 70 kinds of relish, 15 brands of green beans, and 25 checkouts— only 5 of which may be open at any one time. That's quite all right with Trader Joe's. The company has never strived to be the weekly store for the typical American family or the minivan-driving soccer mom with three kids in tow and a fist full of coupons for Kraft macaroni-and-cheese and Pringles potato chips. Trader Joe's is quite content to cultivate a quirky image without mainstream appeal.

The company truly is the antithesis of a retail world in which bigger is usually better when it comes to supermarkets. With the average store ranging from 6,000 to 12,000 square feet, a Trader Joe's store is about one-third the size of an average supermarket and, as previously noted, contains only about 10 percent of the usual selection. Any one of its stores could probably fit comfortably inside the sporting goods department of the local Wal-Mart supercenter. The Wal-Mart would also be a lot easier to find, given that Trader Joe's outlets are still relatively scarce in most areas of the country and usually are tucked away in some small, outdated strip shopping center. These unimpressive, aesthetically challenged minimalls are found in every town in the

United States and usually house small local businesses (such as delis and card shops).

With so many negatives, especially at first blush, why and how has Trader Joe's created such a buzz and garnered such a loyal following? Because initial impressions can be deceiving!

Trader Joe's has made a habit of being in the right place at the right time, with the right products at the right price. This is not something that other retailers can't accomplish, but few, if any, have been able to create the kind of fun shopping experience that Trader Joe's provides. Rather than turning people off, these quirky traits excite customers, giving them a unique shopping alternative for their time-crunched lives and ideas for creating interesting new dishes.

BE CHOOSY

Rather than viewing Trader Joe's as small and cramped, customers see it as a cozy and easy-to-shop environment. It is a mecca for gourmet bargain hunters, natural and organic food freaks, and anyone looking for an alternative to the white-bread, cookie-cutter, conventional supermarkets that dot the country. This is not to say that creativity doesn't exist in the industry at large. It's just that Trader Joe's takes it to a different level. The company flourishes by entertaining customers, creating a need for its own array of private label items, and making product choices easier. Remember, the company's strategy calls for offering only one or two choices of each item, so shoppers don't have many options. This strategy has simplified their shopping experience, which elsewhere has become increasingly complex due to the overwhelming variety of products on the shelves.

In some ways, this strategy is similar to Oprah Winfrey's wildly successful book club. When Winfrey selects a title, people read it whether they've heard of the book or not. Likewise, when Trader Joe's says a product is good, people buy it. The chain, much like the book club, edits people's lives by boiling selections down to the essentials—or at least what Trader Joe's considers to be the essentials.

This entire customer experience is the result of smart, gutsy buying and good customer research, all of which enable the chain to cater to new cultural and culinary trends much faster than its conventional counterparts. Then again, don't underestimate Trader Joe's tongue-in-cheek approach to marketing, merchandising, and advertising. By injecting a sense of humor, fun, and reasonable prices into shopping for complex categories like gourmet and health-oriented products, the company removes the anxiety and intimidation consumers feel when shopping other stores. This also enables Trader Joe's to build credibility and trust among consumers in diverse markets—people who may still shop Wal-Mart for price but long for the good old days of the neighborhood grocer who offered a little something different. This company clearly focuses on doing the right thing versus just getting things done.

IGNITE THE IMAGINATION

In this case, the right thing is an environment that fires a customer's imagination. It opens their eyes to culinary possibilities they might never have considered. You can't always do that with a standard supermarket formula and plain vanilla looks. Sometimes it means being a bit sloppy and haphazard. This is where the plastic lobsters and fishnets come in handy. But, according to industry sources, the downscale look is really a brilliant disguise for a company that has made a science out of looking unprofessional. This lets Trader Joe's live securely and profitably in the shadow of far larger chains, which seem to regard the company as merely a gnat on an elephant. Competitors see Trader Joe's as capturing some sales but not enough to worry about compared to a Wal-Mart supercenter, for instance.

As retail industry consultant Kevin Kelley puts it, "They [Trader Joe's] live very close to the moat and people in the castle don't worry about them." That's a big mistake, especially since this gnat-like competitor is clearly biting into the sales of these stores.

For one thing, Trader Joe's is an adept practitioner of "atmospherics," a concept that can be traced back to 1974, when environmental psychologists began studying the impact of environmental factors on people—like the color of the paint in prisons and hospitals. In the 1980s, atmospherics became a hot strategic tool for trendy retailers like Victoria's Secret and Niketown to create new and exciting retail shopping experiences.

"There's an entertainment aspect to retailing. It's all about appealing to a consumer's lifestyle," explains Letty Workman, author, lecturer, and professor of international business at Utah Valley State College. "We have a sporting goods chain here called REI. It's a big playground where you can try out the hiking boots, rock climbing apparel, and accessories on a climbing wall inside the store before you buy. The employees are very informed about the merchandise and all the activities. It ends up involving the consumers at a much higher level. They have fun and stay longer. And the longer they stay in this environment, the higher the probability of purchase."

REI is a lifestyle store where everything is geared to bring customers back. The environment is an extension of who customers are and offers them a chance to express themselves through their purchasing behavior.

Trader Joe's is a perfect model for atmospherics and seems to use it more strategically than other food retailers, both to differentiate itself in the marketplace and to gain customer loyalty. "I have friends in Park City who drive to California. When they do, shopping at Trader Joe's is always one of the highlights of their trip," Workman adds. "Consumers have more options these days. If they don't enjoy a store, they can go elsewhere, including the Internet. Retailers have to give customers another reason to come to the store and go through the trouble of finding a parking space and shopping. Enhancing the entertainment value is one way to do it. This isn't about organic bread. It's about treasure hunting, having fun, and telling people about it."

MAKE IT ADAPTABLE

Interestingly, the chain's entertaining ways had some people thinking that Trader Joe's wouldn't be much of a success outside of California. They felt its quirky appearance and products would appeal primarily to ex-hippies and West Coast liberals—the Birkenstock set. The quintessential Trader Joe's customer, whom we'll examine more closely in the next chapter, has been described as "an out-of-work college professor with a Volvo—an old one."

Still, the formula has translated well in other states, even though it may never be the supermarket of choice in the vast Midwest heartland, the rural South where Wal-Mart is king, or any area with big families that are only interested in specials on national brands. When Trader Joe's made its initial leap across the country to Boston, many locals were already familiar with the chain from visits to California. When the company opened in Chicago, lines of eager shoppers appeared at the door. This demonstrated to even the retailer's harshest skeptics that while Trader Joe's clearly has some demographic boundaries, it really doesn't have any geographic ones.

The company's entertaining approach has provided a valuable lesson for executives who are willing to open their minds and think differently about retail strategy. Granted, the concept will not work for everyone. Few, if any, large chains could pull off a concept like Trader Joe's because of the vast differences in retail estate, distribution, buying, marketing, and merchandising strategies alone. That's one reason why, with the possible exception of Whole Foods Market, Trader Joe's has no real chain competition. Larger companies simply can't replicate the culture, nor do they completely understand how it works. To see this, all you have to do is talk to any retail consultant who takes supermarket clients for regular visits to Trader Joe's stores. "They still don't get it," says one observer shaking his head. "Even after all this time, they see the company as a bunch of left-coast hippies wearing stupid shirts, not as a viable format that shoppers love. Believe me, they're making a big mistake, but Trader Joe's loves that attitude."

The problem with traditional supermarket executives is that they are confusing fact with perception, according to Kevin Kelley. "You have to understand that Trader Joe's is an acquired taste," he notes. "But once people get into it, they start to see it as a weekly hunting trip to find out what's new. People go out of their way to find one cracker that only Trader Joe's sells or to buy their (private label) corn chowder."

While many stores have been remodeled in recent years and upgraded to include such basic amenities as wider aisles, automatic doors, scanners, credit and debit card readers, and slightly more modern graphics, the overall concept has changed very little since the first store opened in Pasadena in 1967. In fact, it would be a huge mistake for the stores to change at all, because change might mean abandoning the very things that made them successful. The stores are a magnet for shoppers who agree that less is more and can't resist coming in for such impulse items as vegetarian pot stickers, organic dog biscuits, or eco-friendly detergents not available anywhere else.

The chain's entertaining style even extends to in-store signage, which is often handwritten in a cheerful and comedic style with brief descriptions for all items, including such cleverly named products as Trader Zen's Foaming Cleanser and Joe's Very American Salad. This evokes a feeling that the store is home to the eclectic, not the usual sterile supermarket environment striving for mass-markct appeal. Even the packaging for its extensive private label lines has a sense of humor. Mexican items like salsas, chimichangas, and burritos are branded under the Trader

José monicker; vitamins and nutritional supplements are packaged under the Trader Darwin label; and Asian and Italian fare come under the Trader Ming and Trader Giotto tags, respectively.

BUILD YOUR BRAND WITH A HUMAN TOUCH

Keep in mind that this clever style is not just about selling products. By using unique names and its trademark approach, Trader Joe's is building its brand—striving to be some things to some people. In effect, it is using a retailing rifle shot in place of a scattergun approach. The result is that while people go to conventional supermarkets intent on getting out as soon as possible, a trip to Trader Joe's is an opportunity to linger in an environment that welcomes browsers. If you buy, so much the better—especially for the company's prodigiously healthy balance sheet. But the environment, a limited but unusual product line, and customer-friendly staff are all geared to fulfill one question: Are you having fun?

The mix of these elements—music, decorations, eccentric labels, clever advertising, samples, cheerful employees, and low prices—makes the difference. It's also a major reason that trying to copy Trader Joe's operating style is a failing proposition for would-be competitors. "It's not about the mechanistic—or the machinery—of Trader Joe's that makes it so wildly successful," claims retail consultant Gretchen Gogesch. "It's because they focus on the human side of the equation." Large companies, whether they sell groceries or clothing, are really fancified cousins of the industrial age and the thinking that came out of that era. To them, it's all about quantity and getting enough bodies in the store to take products off the shelves. "But this is just delivering commodities, not engaging customers," Gogesch points out. "Delivering this proposition takes a special vision. In the mainstream, you don't find that vision in any industry, and they don't teach it in business schools. As a culture we measure numbers."

Founder Joe Coulombe focused on what made people passionately happy when they walked into his stores. It's he who best personified the company's vision. The products made people happy and lifted them out of their otherwise routine, everyday experiences. Then there's the matter of trust, something that can only be built by being genuine and coming through with the payoff. Other companies talk a good game about being consumercentric but don't really deliver on the promise when you go into the store.

Years ago, the legendary advertising man David Ogilvy said, "The customer is not stupid. She's your wife. Look across the kitchen table to get an idea of who you're serving." Trader Joe's pulls it off because they are authentic and instill passion for the consumer in every store. Safeway or other retailers can try to knock the company off, but they can't. The concept fails if you don't focus on people. This isn't about putting something on the retail shelf. It's about what's in the human heart.

It's part and parcel of what's been called the Trader Joe's culture—something the chain wears on its sleeve like a badge of honor. It's something very difficult for the average large U.S. organization to replicate. Trader Joe's is extremely focused on what it is and what it is about. As one industry observer noted, "It's all about being prepared but relaxed, knowing but never condescending, clever but not trendy. The culture dips into the health food movement; the gourmet food, wine, and booze craze; and the ever-popular discount ideal. But all in moderation."[1] Bill Bishop, a retail industry consultant, puts it this way: "When was the last time you voluntarily went out to browse in a supermarket? People browse at Trader Joe's."

Libby Sartaine, former head of human resources for Southwest Airlines and now a vice president of human resources for Yahoo, is a loyal Trader Joe's customer who exemplifies this trait. "I've become a regular [customer] since moving to California. I love them, and I can't live without them now. They have so many things I didn't know I needed." Sartaine admits to being addicted to the store's frozen tofu bars and buying six or eight boxes at a time. The only negative? "It's so crowded on weekends that you can't just stroll through and enjoy it."

Then there's the story of the woman in Cambridge, Massachusetts, who was among dozens who lined up to get into a new Trader Joe's as soon as it opened. When the doors were finally unlocked she grabbed a cart and ran up and down the aisles shouting, "Yahoo!" When was the last time you saw a customer at your local grocery store do that?

CREATE RAVING FANS

On its own somewhat irreverent Web site, the company relishes the idea that some customers call the stores "the home of cheap thrills." Such a comment is typical of the company's devotees, who often lobby local politicians as well as Trader Joe's itself to get a store built in their neighborhood. Part of the attraction is that, like them, the company doesn't take itself too seriously. How could you, when the store is built around a tropical theme with background music that has been described as a combination of the Beach Boys, Seattle grunge, and National Public Radio?[2] This seems to fit in an environment where store employees wear Hawaiian shirts and are referred to as captains, first mates, and crew.

One thing you'll notice is that Trader Joe's stores look pretty much the same whether you're in Emeryville, California, or Hicksville, New York. The consistency of store design and limited selection of high-quality organic and gourmet items at discount prices attracts people to Trader Joe's and keeps them coming back, even if the nearest store is 25 miles away.

As noted, the chain doesn't satisfy everyone's weekly shopping needs and was never meant to. It does represent a more personal shopping experience for those willing to make an additional trip to their neighborhood supermarket for things like fresh meat, brand-name groceries, and a larger selection of produce. The more intimate environment at Trader Joe's may be even more popular in years to come, as affluent baby boomers with active lifestyles and a yen for something different abandon or at least cut back on visits to traditional supermarkets. Then there are those shoppers who are simply tired of making the trek up and down the aisles of their local 60,000-square-foot store for the same old stuff.

EMPHASIZE WHAT'S NEW

If there's one thing that sets Trader Joe's apart from the rest of the food retailing field, it's not having the same old thing. In fact, the reason it appeals so much to shoppers is that emphasis on the new and different. And even with a limited number of products, Trader Joe's offers shoppers a better selection than mainstream supermarkets. "You're giving consumers a choice if you just stock one blueberry juice instead of ten varieties of Coca-Cola. Customers go there because they don't need ten choices of the same old thing," according to one marketing consultant.

Trader Joe's has joined the ranks of retailers who appeal to the shopper's need for differentiation. This retail group is pretty small and includes Whole Foods Market and Costco warehouse clubs. In fact, some believe that Costco has a lot in common with Trader Joe's, even though they are arguably at different ends of the retail spectrum. Both have recognized the true value of private labeling and the need to offer a little surprise every time you turn a corner. As one California shopper noted, "When was the last time you had fun shopping at Safeway?"

This mind-set goes back to the days when founder Joe Coulombe cherry-picked discontinued merchandise and overstocks from gourmet food manufacturers and local wine distributors. These ever-changing closeouts were partly responsible for turning the shopping experience at Trader Joe's into recreation.

Of course, any discussion of fun shopping would be incomplete without mentioning Two-Buck Chuck, the line of cheap wine produced under the Charles Shaw label and available exclusively at Trader Joe's. These "extreme value" wines became the fastest-growing label in history when customers began hauling it out of the stores by the caseload.[3] It became a badge of honor—a little secret shared by loyal Trader Joe's shoppers—and a conversation piece at every Christmas and New Year's celebration across the country. We'll take a look in Chapter 8 at how this wine phenomenon came about.

STAY SOCIALLY CORRECT

Sometimes fun at Trader Joe's translates into social and ecological correctness. The company has very carefully cultivated a reputation not only for the unusual but also for how its products are made. Items purchased under the Trader Joe's label do not include genetically modified ingredients. When an animal rights group complained that ducks were being slaughtered inhumanely, the chain stopped selling packages of refrigerated duck breasts. The ahi tuna (even the cat food variety) is caught without nets to protect the dolphins, the dried apricots are unsulfered, and the peanut butter is organic.[4] Customers also like the idea that the company is active in local food donation programs, giving away 30 to 60 gallons of items every day.

This brand of social activism is evident as soon as you enter the store and see an entire wall devoted to brochures and pamphlets on Fair Trade coffee, everything you wanted to know about soy foods, and a complete list of all items in the store that qualify as organic. Additional flyers focus on fat, calorie, and fiber content; give a detailed explanation of rennet—the milk-clotting enzyme in cheese; and outline kosher foods, low-sodium and sodium-free items, and the no-sugar added and gluten-free products in every department. Few retailers offer such detailed health and diet information.

Along with this, Trader Joe's stores have blackboard-style signs that discuss various food issues, like how long an unopened canned product can be stored before spoiling or defining such terms as trans-fatty acids and explaining what monodiglycerides are.

BE FEARLESS IN YOUR ADVERTISING

With the exception of some sporadic radio spots, Trader Joe's doesn't advertise in traditional media. The radio ads, as always, are done on the cheap and in the same friendly, down-home style as everything else. The weekly, screaming, promotional price-based ads favored by most supermarkets simply wouldn't work for Trader Joe's. Instead, the chain produces the informative yet tongue-in-cheek *Fearless Flyer* newsletter. Conventional wisdom says that slick television and print advertising is necessary for building a brand. The *Fearless Flyer* is about as far as you can get from that. This monthly publication usually runs about 24 pages and is sometimes described as a cross between *Consumer Reports* and *Mad* magazine. Its old-fashioned graphics are straight out of a Victorian primer with a bit of Monty Python thrown in for good measure.

Still, the *Fearless Flyer* is an extremely effective sales and promotional tool. It not only offers the latest products and prices but also extols the virtues of each item in a way that makes you feel as though you're doing the wrong thing if you don't buy it. For example, a recent issue waxed poetic over black peppered cashews from Thailand's island resort of Phuket—even telling readers how it's pronounced (foo-ket).

Then there was the organic soycutash ("sufferin' soycutash—this isn't your same old mixed vegetable blend"). While the product may have indeed been a great buy at $1.99 for 16 ounces, the ad infused a little poetry into the sales pitch, telling readers, "It's aesthetically interesting with its many vibrant hues."

If you want to know about Trader José's guacamole, the *Fearless Flyer* will inform you that it's produced in a state-of-the-art plant, only yards away from an avocado grove. And, in a bow to the health-conscious, the newsletter notes that the guacamole has no preservatives or sulfites and is packed in nitrogen-flushed tubs to preserve freshness. This may be more than you want to know, but it's in keeping with Trader Joe's informative and entertaining style.

Trader Joe's is not above sprinkling a few well-placed bad puns throughout the *Fearless Flyer*. Among those in a recent issue: a bettah feta . . . a grill's best friend . . . soy vay marinades . . . olive the nightlife . . . and get thee to a bunnery.

Marketing consultant Phyllis Ezop says the closest thing to the *Fearless Flyer* is probably the *Michelin Guide,* although it doesn't have as many bad puns. Michelin started with tires but also promotes travel and provides interesting facts about things people find along the highways and byways—much the same as Trader Joe's does for its products.

While the *Fearless Flyer* creates an unusual and memorable experience for shoppers, there's a more serious reason for Trader Joe's lack of traditional advertising—the cost. There's an old saying on Madison Avenue that half of all advertising is wasted—it's just that no one knows which half! The company does some public radio spots in new markets, but the *Fearless Flyer* has enabled the company to pretty much cut out the waste inherent in national and regional advertising campaigns by being available only to people in the store or through the mail by special request. This makes Trader Joe's one of the most effective—and entertaining—direct marketers in the country.

CHAPTER 5

Know Your Target Customer

S o, who are Trader Joe's customers, and what exactly are they looking for? It's a question that elicits numerous interesting answers—many of which seem to be somewhat tongue in cheek, more suited to David Letterman's top-ten list than a serious discussion about consumer research. Among those cited by both the company and industry analysts are the following:

- Out-of-work PhD's
- College professors who drive Volvos—old ones (the Volvos, not the professors!)
- The overeducated and underpaid
- Health-conscious label readers
- People with champagne tastes and beer incomes
- Social and political activists
- Well-read, well-traveled people who appreciate a good value
- An eclectic assortment of foodies, college students, sugar fiends, and health nuts[1]

- Yuppie epicures in search of Tasmanian feta cheese; carrot ginger dressing; and organic, flourless, sprouted seven-grain bread[2]

Customers of Trader Joe's have also been described as people who wear their disdain for national brand food items like a badge of honor, have the ability to tolerate Greenpeace solicitors, wear sunscreen over their tattoos, travel on frequent-flier miles, play guitars, pay their taxes, Rollerblade or bike to work when they're not driving the minivan, and dress their kids in tie-dye. "Such folks might have unfortunate thoughts about their fellow Americans while waiting in the sun for a parking place, but they would never, ever yell at them out the window."[3]

Scarborough Research, which measures lifestyle and shopping patterns, says the typical Trader Joe's customer in the Pacific Northwest is a college-educated, white homeowner with a median age of 44 and a median household income of $64,000. Customers are almost evenly divided among married and singles, females and males, but about two-thirds have no kids at home.[4]

The chain's vice president of marketing and chief spokesperson, Pat St. John, would likely agree. As you can imagine, Trader Joe's knows its target customer well. St. John has described them as cost-conscious and health-conscious label readers who aren't tied to national brands. Company surveys have also found that many customers are well traveled and looking to replicate foods they have enjoyed elsewhere.[5] Of course, it doesn't hurt that store employees are constantly talking to customers.

Moreover, globalization of the entire food industry is making unique products more available than they once were, and consumers are anxious to try new taste sensations from a wide variety of ethnic and multicultural cuisines. Trader Joe's has become expert at mining these cultural trends and boils them down to a few simple choices, which usually involve one of the company's private label products.

CREATE YOUR OWN CULTURE

Frankly, little has changed since the chain's inception on the West Coast during the 1960s. Trader Joe's quirky environment and eclectic products have always attracted a more highly educated group of customers. But by appealing to a certain lifestyle rather than particular customers, it has done what few other food retailers have accomplished—created its own culture and appealed to a unique demographic.

The people who buy into this culture are not really hardcore health food freaks, wine snobs, or upscale shoppers, as some believe. They represent a new demographic that is attracted to the middle ground—moderates who like all-natural foods, but not too much; the diet-conscious, who enjoy regular indulgences; and wannabe oenophiles who love the idea of discovering a hidden gem among cases of inexpensive wines.

If Trader Joe's has targeted one specific consumer group, it may represent the biggest one out there—disaffected supermarket shoppers looking for something different in a consumer-friendly environment. These customers dread the weekly shopping trip and see it as a boring, expensive chore that ranks right up there with going to the dry cleaners or dentist. Every mainstream supermarket basically offers the same products in the same general configuration, and pricing is virtually the same everywhere, because retailers pretty much get identical deals and promotional allowances from manufacturers.

To combat this malaise, supermarkets have continued to build larger stores, add more products, hold more sales, and institute anemic discounts on groceries by requiring customers to join frequent shopper programs—a strategy that has, for the most part, failed to win the hearts and minds of shoppers. Trader Joe's doesn't have any kind of formal frequent shopper program and, if history is any guide, probably won't ever start one. Here, consumer loyalty is not a matter of offering discounts or reward points, and any attempt to institute such a program would do little, if anything, to increase store traffic. If there is a frequent shopper program, it lies in the chain's ability to surprise customers with interesting new items every week. This strategy creates frequent shoppers.

Without question, the Trader Joe's customer is not overly concerned by the following:

- Small stores
- Narrow aisles
- Limited selection
- Lack of parking
- No national brands
- Absence of weekly hot specials.

All of this makes for interesting speculation and memorable descriptions. But to understand who Trader Joe's customers are and why they admire the store so much, you have to speak with them directly. We asked several shoppers in the New York area to offer their views on the chain and why they like it. Here are some of their responses.

- *Patricia of Hicksville, New York, 52, medical billing assistant, married mother of two boys (ages 16 and 20).* "I've been shopping at Trader Joe's every couple of weeks or so for about two years. I work full-time, and I don't have time to cook meals every day. I still go to the supermarket for a lot of things. But I buy a lot of frozen foods and meals here, like the Mexican stuff for my sons and the fish or the Greek pizza for my husband and me. I also got addicted to the chocolate cat cookies. I think prices are cheaper here than at the supermarket, and I like the quality of pretty much everything."
- *Sidney (retired dry cleaner) and Helen (homemaker) of Long Beach, New York, both in their 70s.* Sidney: "I'm supposed to watch my diet, and this is all healthy stuff. I like the whole

grain bread, the milk tastes fresher, and if my wife leaves me alone, I sometimes get the big chunks of chocolate they have in the baskets. But it's hard to get a parking spot." Helen: "It's just the two of us now, so I don't cook much. I like the small packages of hamburgers. I tried the buffalo, too. He didn't like it, but I did. I also buy the all-natural skin moisturizers. We come here maybe once a week to look around. We don't always buy something, but it's fun to just look, and everybody that works here is so nice."

- *Tabitha of Valley Stream, New York, 27, advertising sales representative, single.* "I work in Manhattan during the week, so I usually come in on weekends for some things I can keep in the freezer for quick, easy meals. It's a pretty small store, so it doesn't take a lot of my time. I like the yogurt, the different kinds of potato chips, and the salsas. My boyfriend loves the Trader Joe's root beer, too. It's always interesting to see what you can find. I have a cat, so I buy the natural snacks and dry cat food."

It's important to note that none of these people shop exclusively at Trader Joe's. They are all at the supermarket at least once a week and usually twice for fill-in items—particularly meat and produce, which are not really the focus of Trader Joe's. These are not a bunch of aging hippies whose youthful excesses are turning into middle-aged malaise. Nor are they particularly overeducated—at least from a formal schooling point of view. Granted, these opinions come from only a handful of people in one area of the country. But it does raise an interesting question: are all the stereotypes that even the company puts out about its customers actually real? In other words, does Trader Joe's legitimately focus on a particular type of customer, or are they simply trying to perpetuate a mystique? After all, the illusion that something is only meant for certain people draws everyone in to check out the hoopla.

It is interesting that a chain where national brands and advertising are virtually nonexistent has gathered such a loyal and varied following. One reason is that because Trader Joe's itself is the brand, dedicated and admiring shoppers spread the word for free on behalf of the company.

Such admiration is apparent in many places, including the Internet. For example, http://www.Lovemarks.com is a research and survey tool developed by the advertising firm Saatchi & Saatchi. The site enables users to post opinions, give feedback, or nominate their favorite brands. It's a brand manager's dream or nightmare, depending on the responses. A quick search on the site revealed some interesting comments by Trader Joe's customers about why they shop at the store.[6]

- *Adele.* "A trip to Trader Joe's is as fun and full of adventure as a trip to Disneyland. There's always something new and wonderful to discover and taste. I refuse to live in any city that's more than 30 minutes away from a Trader Joe's."
- *Cherilyn.* "It has the best selection and prices on gourmet and healthy foods. I love trying out new food and beverage flavor combinations each time I shop."
- *Gill.* "Trader Joe's is extraordinary. It's an exquisite oasis for savoring the benefits of healthy foods. The almonds I recently bought at Trader Joe's are incredible—the best I've ever had. The store is exceptionally colorful, from the product displays to the aloha shirts worn by the employees . . . The samples on my last visit alone were worth the trip. The flowers available for sale could rival those in a conservatory, and the skin care products are fragrant and soothing."
- *Lisa.* "The only problem with Trader Joe's is that there aren't enough of them. I have to drive a half hour to get to the nearest one. But it's worth it. The frozen entrees are great, and I buy lots of different kinds of nuts and dried fruit."

- *David (from the United Kingdom).* "I spent a number of years in San Diego, and Trader Joe's was the place to go. I would love to see them in the UK—on second thought, I'll go back to California."
- *Callipygian.* "What about Two-Buck Chuck? This $2 wine revolutionized the wine market. When consumers realized a good bottle of wine was available for such a great price, they scrambled, buying cases and cases . . . Vive la revolution! Down with overpriced wine."
- *Clive.* "It's a yuppie grocery store with eclectic upmarket prices set in a funky warehouse-style setting and discount prices . . . It's the kind of store you're introduced to by friends and coworkers when you move into the neighborhood, as if you were being offered membership to a special club with privileged knowledge."

There's no doubt that, at one time, there was a "typical" Trader Joe's customer. Some of the aforementioned comments seem to indicate that this is still true. No doubt Trader Joe's is also never going to be America's supermarket or the breadbasket of the heartland. Even if the chain eventually expands to some 2,000 stores around the United States—a number cited by several industry experts—it will never be the supermarket of choice for large families, bulk buyers, or coupon addicts. To become that would mean stocking the usual selection of national brands and bringing in more meat and produce. Trader Joe's will never do these things—nor should it. Yet it continues to have an extremely loyal customer base.

DRAW CUSTOMERS TO YOU

Over the past 20 years or so, *customer loyalty* has become an oxymoron in the supermarket industry. Customers are no longer tied to one store the way previous generations were. Their shopping habits are based primarily on convenience, selection, and price—the latter changing from week to week depending on specials. Even the spate of loyalty programs that have cropped up in recent years have largely failed to keep customers happy with one store for very long. And the discount cards and key chains that bulk up the average person's wallet have become less of an attraction and more of an annoyance for customers who see very little, if any, difference between most stores.

Because of some recent changes at Trader Joe's, some are asking whether the chain is changing its stripes to appeal to a more mainstream customer, or whether the mainstream customer is merely being drawn into the Trader Joe's culture. The answer is that, to a minor degree, the stores are changing. Private labels still represent the bulk of the product mix. Private labels attract people to Trader Joe's, and the company is not about to abandon the principles that made it successful in the first place. But more regional and even some nationally known brands find their way onto the company's shelves than did ten years ago. Stores are also stocking more meat and produce. The latter, according to industry research, is often the reason consumers choose to shop a particular food market. A good produce department can often spell the difference between a grocer's success and failure.

CREATE A NEED

Still, while there's no doubt Trader Joe's knows its target customer well, it has never prided itself in just giving people what they want. If that were the case, founder Joe Coulombe would have kept Pronto going as a convenience store chain back in the 1960s, prospering on beer, cigarettes, magazines, and the usual staples. Rather, Trader Joe's success lies in *creating* need. After all, how many people really have an inner desire for organic vodka sauce? Creating a need is also a matter of cultivating an image that fits the lifestyles of your customers. In the case of Trader Joe's, it means focusing on things like health issues and making donations to food banks and other causes in which its customers are involved. It's also a matter of being politically correct when necessary, e.g., steering clear of products containing genetically modified organisms (GMOs), dropping meat suppliers using inhumane methods, or stocking only dolphin-safe tuna. This strategy in itself will not attract a broad spectrum of customers to the store. But it does target a specific niche and painlessly makes existing customers feel they are being politically correct by doing something for humanity and the environment.

When Coulombe founded what was to become Trader Joe's, he didn't plan for political correctness or to target upscale consumers per se. Convenience stores do not normally attract the carriage trade. Instead, he was looking for people who lacked income but nonetheless had more expensive, worldlier tastes than the average shopper does. He catered to them with products they couldn't find in their local supermarket. Typically, these people measured high in areas like education and travel. They came back from foreign travels with a more sophisticated palate and began frequenting gourmet shops that specialized in some of the items they had tried while traveling. But they quickly discovered that the pricing in gourmet shops was pretty much out of reach, especially because they got the same items at a fraction of the cost during their travels. What they wanted was gourmet and international foods at discount prices. Before Trader Joe's came on the scene, finding this combination was almost impossible.

TRACK SALES FROM MANY PERSPECTIVES

Coulombe didn't just track the number of items that were selling, he also looked at what purchases were being made, when, and by whom. Then, as now, detailed consumer research was an important part of the Trader Joe's strategy. In most instances, so-called standard research with a clipboard and a set of questions is both valid and necessary to any business. In fact, many food industry observers will freely admit that traditional supermarkets would be in better shape if they simply asked customers what they wanted instead of dictating what stores sell. But just asking questions is not enough to find out who your customer is. Standard research doesn't tell you what you don't ask. This makes it difficult to pick up on the nuances of consumer needs. While Trader Joe's is not always 100 percent on target when it comes to identifying and understanding its customers, the chain remains light-years ahead of larger mainstream supermarket chains, which are largely ineffective in their efforts to target specific customer groups—including those who shop at Trader Joe's and similar competitors.

PRACTICE ANTHROPOLOGY

Observational research has become Trader Joe's stock-in-trade over the years. Coulombe was a pioneer in tracking how consumer behavior translated into purchasing, making him one of the first retail anthropologists. Anthropology can take the place of surveys, questionnaires, and even focus groups and is often more accurate.

Category management is now common practice among retailers, particularly for supermarkets, which are inundated with thousands and thousands of new products each year (80 to 90 percent of which fail). Trader Joe's certainly tracks sales in particular categories. But it goes beyond that into the realm of understanding how people spend their leisure time, what they do on vacation, and what they're reading. This is the essence of retail anthropology. An outgrowth of that, however, has been the development of 360-degree marketing, which is not just understanding customers' behavior but also what makes them tick.

As retail industry consultant Gretchen Gogesch puts it, "They [Trader Joe's] like to keep an eye on the whole customer and view them from a very holistic point of view. To them, the customer is not just a sale at the cash register. They are part of Trader Joe's powerful research and development teams."

In this way, Trader Joe's is not asking customers to adjust to what the store wants to sell—a strategy used by most supermarket chains. Instead, it tries to understand how Trader Joe's can fit into customers' lives and lifestyles. This enables the chain to ferret out "hot spots" among the customer base, which it can marry to create winning products.

This, by the way, is believed to have originally influenced Coulombe to choose a tropical theme for the store interiors. He was an astute people watcher and decided that travel and vacations were big with his customers. This observation led him to create a fun environment that was full of great products at prices that didn't make people feel like paupers.

The company also has the wisdom to let the marketplace and consumers dictate what goes into which stores. For example, you might be able to get Dr. Bronner's Peppermint Soap in Mountain View, California, but not necessarily in Chicago or Phoenix. The same goes for regional foods that simply don't appeal to everyone, everywhere. Sometimes customer comment cards will determine which products make it to the shelves at Trader Joe's—or at least what products the company's buyers should look for.

LISTEN AND RESPOND TO FEEDBACK

Customer comment cards and the old suggestion box are almost as old as the supermarket industry itself. More often than not, store managers would empty the box when it got too full and, depending on what kind of day they were having, look at the comments or throw them into the trash. Today, the same thing is generally still true. At best, contents of the old suggestion box are dumped into the lap of some temp to input into the company computer and promptly be forgotten. It's the electronic version of the wastebasket.

But at Trader Joe's, customer comments—whether by card or directly to store employees—are taken very seriously by both executives at headquarters and by store managers, who are made aware of all comments on an ongoing basis. They are not about to be relegated to the garbage bin, because customer satisfaction is built into a manager's incentive program.

Besides, who wouldn't want to satisfy a customer who might have traveled 25 miles to get to a Trader Joe's store and who expects it to be nothing less than a journey of discovery and recreation? Former customers who no longer live near a Trader Joe's have been known to pack an extra carry-on bag on cross-country trips so they can bring home Trader Joe's products. However far away they may be from the store, these customers like to voice their opinions about all manner of things—and they like to be heard. Take the residents of Davis, California, who have a penchant for political, environmental, and social activism. They sent a petition to Trader Joe's CEO, Dan Bane, and the vice president of marketing, Pat St. John, in May 2004, lobbying for a store to open in that community. The petition outlined Davis's demographics and its considerable purchasing power, and it compared local incomes to other California college towns in which Trader Joe's operates—all with footnotes. Despite the effort, Davis has yet to get a store. The nearest locations seem to be in Sacramento and Roseville, both of which are 20 miles or more from this college town.

With rare exceptions, supermarkets do not elicit this kind of emotional investment by consumers. Just ask Wal-Mart, whose plans to open football field–sized stores in California and elsewhere have been met with jeers, not cheers, by residents and municipalities, whose battle cry has become NIMBY—Not In My Back Yard!

ENCOURAGE BROWSING

As Trader Joe's goes into new markets and more people experience the company's culture, stores will continue to attract a customer base as eclectic as the products on the shelves—everyone from working mothers and 20-something singles to baby boomers and seniors.

What Trader Joe's represents is a lifestyle store—an extension of who the shopper really wants to be. And what they want to be when visiting the store is health-conscious—without the pain of deprivation—and a gourmand—without spending too much. This lifestyle retailing invites people to stay longer and browse. Everything in a traditional supermarket is geared to get customers through as quickly as possible to increase turnover. Trader Joe's wants people to stop, read the signs and bad jokes, pick up the product, read the label, and talk about it. The stores are every marketer's dream—an event and experience people can collectively share. To a degree, Trader Joe's is the culmination of work begun by environmental psychologists in the early 1970s, which, over the past decade, evolved into the science of atmospherics.

In effect, it is teaching people to shop differently and showing them that the terms *gourmet* and *bargain* are not mutually exclusive. In many ways, Trader Joe's is doing for its customers what warehouse club stores like Costco do on a much bigger scale.

But Trader Joe's strategy lies in not caring that a portion of the population won't shop in its stores. This is far different from mainstream supermarkets that get caught in "the mushy middle" by trying to be everything to everybody. With Trader Joe's, targeting customers is a matter of going narrow and deep. The company has done better than virtually any other chain in sticking to its strategic guns.

Trader Joe's unique accomplishment is teaching its audience to move toward it, instead of the other way around. The chain has become the arbiter of taste and culinary style in a non-threatening and nonintimidating package—a magnet for people who shop the store almost exclusively, as well as those occasional visitors drawn in for something special. Subconsciously, consumers know that if it's on the shelf and Trader Joe's puts its name on it, the item has got to be good.

NEVER LOSE SIGHT OF STRATEGY

There's no doubt that Trader Joe's—despite its size, or perhaps because of it—has expertly identified and catered to its target customers. The question is whether this strategy can be kept up in the future. The key will be to continue this strategy as it expands, while avoiding being seduced into broadening its field of fire. One might argue that Whole Foods is starting to fall into this trap, by trying to be more like a traditional grocery store to reap the benefits of Wall Street. Because Trader Joe's is a private company and no doubt wants to stay that way, customer strategy is likely to be remain untarnished.

The idea of becoming a publicly traded company is probably a moot point, because Aldi and the Albrecht family like their personal and business privacy. Going public would require a mountain of financial and operational disclosures—anathema for a company that has zealously shunned the spotlight. The company can't stand talking to local news reporters, let alone receiving the third degree that would come from detail-hungry financial analysts. More to the point, going public would place Trader Joe's under the myopic lens of Wall Street, which believes that companies are only as strong as their latest quarterly earnings. A public company pretty much has to satisfy Wall Street analysts to survive, and that often means abandoning creativity and innovation—the traits that have endeared Trader Joe's to legions of customers.

GET INTIMATE

Trader Joe's is pretty much in the zone when it comes to feeding the consumer's palate and expectations. Despite the success of Wal-Mart and other big-box behemoths, the American public is shunning the mass market for more intimate buying experiences. Even the venerable Procter & Gamble, which defined mass marketing for the past century, is changing its stripes. The company, whose burgeoning portfolio consists of such mass-market darlings as Tide, Crest, and Pampers, insists that its brands are not mass market but targeted toward millions of particular consumers. James Stengel, Procter & Gamble's global marketing officer, explains the way it works: "You find people; you are very focused on them; you become relevant to them."[7] The story is the same for many other major corporations. McDonald's only devotes one-third of its marketing budget to television, compared with two-thirds five years ago. Now the focus is on its target audience, like young males, which can be reached more effectively through ads on the in-store video network at Footlocker. By contrast, they can reach young mothers through ads in *O,* Oprah Winfrey's magazine. The same strategy is evident at many other mass marketers, which, interestingly enough, are now practicing the kind of cultural anthropology to target consumers that Trader Joe's has used almost since its inception.

Working to the advantage of Trader Joe's is that the supermarket industry at large may be the last bastion of mass marketing. For years the industry has been talking about target marketing and abandoning the one-size-fits-all approach to food retailing. When consumers have more choices than ever—from traditional stores as well as online shops—retailers can scarcely afford to turn their backs on customers for even a second. It is simply too easy for consumers to head down the block to the local convenience store, drugstore, or discounter to pick up grocery staples and then head to Trader Joe's for something special. Again, consumer research is not a matter of chasing the latest food fad but understanding deeply rooted human needs and desires. This goes beyond the superficial findings of focus groups into the realm of retail anthropology and social science to observe consumer behavior and root out unfulfilled needs.

Many retailers hoped that a loyalty card or frequent shopper program would give them enough information on shoppers to change the way they do business. The reality is that shoppers are forced to collect the cards to get a nominal discount on groceries, and retailers, while collecting customer data, are letting it collect dust rather than analyzing and acting on it.

The previous statement is a broad stroke and may not apply to every supermarket out there. However, as noted earlier, using information to target customer needs or create products they didn't know they wanted is Trader Joe's stock-in-trade. Letting this information languish on someone's desk just isn't done. As long as the company pays attention to the information it gathers and enhances customer loyalty through innovative new products and strong customer service, a growing army of loyal shoppers will flock to its stores no matter where they are.

As Kevin Costner's character in the movie *Field of Dreams* is told, "If you build it [and build it right], they will come."

CHAPTER 6

Always Deliver Value

Value: *"An amount regarded as a suitable equivalent for something else; a fair price or return for goods and services."*
—Webster's dictionary

This definition adequately—albeit somewhat clinically—describes what has become one of the most important elements in business today—delivering value to consumers. It is even more important in the front lines of retailing and, specifically, for supermarkets, where competitors are fighting tooth and nail for every penny of the consumer's food dollar. But what really constitutes value in the real world these days? Are retailers making it part of their core competency, or is it just so much lip service? How should it be defined, and where does Trader Joe's fall in the retail value continuum?

There are, admittedly, a lot of questions related to this issue. And if you ask different people, you get different answers. In reality, relatively few good practitioners of the art of offering good customer service exist, while a virtual army simply talks the talk without walking the walk. Billionaire investor Warren Buffett, the sage from Omaha and the icon of every business school graduate, put it this way: "Price is what you pay; value is what you get."

Some have tried to offer both with mixed success. Nearly 150 years ago, legendary retailer Frank W. Woolworth personified the idea of consumer value by melding both value and price into what became one of the most successful retail concepts in history—the five-and-dime store. Woolworth and other retail icons had their day and have since passed into the history books. Meanwhile, the search for value continues unabated, and more confusing solutions seem to abound than ever.

Value can be the legendary customer service offered by companies like Southwest Airlines and Nordstrom's as well as the price gambit played so expertly by JetBlue and Wal-Mart. The latter's origins in the rural south and its journey to become the world's largest retailer—and company—in all of America is the stuff of legend. It certainly makes Sam Walton a more than worthy successor to F. W. Woolworth. As we will discuss, Trader Joe's founder, Joe Coulombe, and his successors, while not on the same scale in terms of size, certainly belong in this category when it comes to operating philosophy.

In the past 20 years, value has become the hallmark of the Japanese automotive industry. It moved from a price-only strategy to focus largely on quality—a path taken by many in the retail industry as well. Value is a key part of the "cheap chic" image developed by Target, a company that has combined quality, fashion merchandising, and low prices into one retail package. Additionally, the value image is also at the center of Wal-Mart and Costco's ability to convince the consuming public that their best interest lies in shopping their stores at least once a week, rather than just visiting the stores once a month to fill up a cart. Similarly, Trader Joe's, which is rarely the primary supermarket for any shopper, has convinced people that it's smart to come back more often because of all the new items that come in weekly—most of them private label items that can't be obtained anywhere else.

These are among the scores of companies across many industries that have become premier value players—those able to change the nature of competition by transforming consumer attitudes towards price and quality and continually improving upon relationships with shoppers.

Of course, just as many companies have failed to optimize value among consumers. Interestingly, Woolworth was hoisted on its own petard when consumers no longer saw the value of the stores and flocked to a new breed of aggressive discounters like Wal-Mart, a raft of dollar stores, and a new generation of drug-stores like Walgreen's and CVS—both of which have successfully cracked the market for low-priced, general merchandise items. Basically, value creation goes astray when companies think they can manipulate consumer demand to suit what they carry, rather than trying to understand what consumers really want.

SEARCH FOR VALUE

Despite a somewhat cyclical economy and the normal ups and downs of consumer confidence, consumers have made an obvious and steady shift in recent years to all kinds of value propositions. This shift cuts across all ages and nearly all income groups.[1]

Shopping at a value-oriented retailer is no longer an activity consumers do every couple of months to make ends meet. It is something that people do every week or more, because their expectations and reference points for both quality and price have fundamentally changed. For instance, value retailers like Target and Kohl's have changed the dynamics of the marketplace by increasing the consumer's access to higher-quality brand-name goods at strong price points, according to a study by McKinsey & Company. At the same time, a retailer like Target is continually upgrading its store brand items. This strategy has enabled the Minnesota-based company to move beyond price as a point of differentiation, something that Kmart—also one of the original value retailers—has failed to do.

Trader Joe's no doubt falls into this group on several fronts. At the core are value-added products and a value-added shopping experience. These things are manifested in everything from private label offerings to store size to employee attitudes. Value is simply a part of this chain's DNA and will stay with it forever— or until someone tries to change it. Given the nature of the business and the management style of both Trader Joe's and its parent company, this seems unlikely to happen any time soon. To resurrect a timeworn phrase—you don't want to kill the goose that lays the golden egg. On the other hand, it's not unheard of for executives—who should know better—to try fixing something that isn't broken.

OFFER MORE

Joe Coulombe's original vision for Trader Joe's was simply to offer more adventurous consumers what they couldn't get elsewhere—gourmet and imported food and wine at prices that wouldn't empty their wallets and would keep them coming back on a weekly basis—not to do their entire shopping but for a little treasure hunting.

But treasure, too, is in the eye of the beholder. To some observers, Trader Joe's is not really value driven in the conventional sense. Consultant and architect Kevin Kelley notes, "It's really only a perception that you save money at Trader Joe's. The secret no one wants to talk about is that it's not that cheap. You might save money on mineral water, but you'll pay it back in other areas like meat. On the other hand, I haven't seen a Trader Joe's in the country that isn't doing some impressive business."

Whether Trader Joe's qualifies as a value retailer in terms of price remains to be seen. But no answer can be found in a vacuum. The company's ability to deliver value to consumers must be viewed in the larger context of whether, and how, the nation's 30,000-plus supermarkets are themselves delivering a clear and consistent value proposition.

To do so, let's look at things from an historical perspective. In some ways, the concept of retail value is the same today as it was a century ago. Great-grandma wanted fresh, high-quality food at the right price—and she wanted it every day. But life was simpler back then. Sirloin was 10 cents a pound, the average wage was 22 cents an hour, and you could buy a house from the Sears and Roebuck catalog for $1,300. There was the neighborhood grocer, the butcher, and the baker. They all knew your name and had what you wanted—or at least what they could provide—and the idea of a store the size of an airplane hangar was inconceivable. After all, if you needed something really special, the grocer could always order it for you.

So much for nostalgia. Fast-forward a century, and the mega-retailers have taken over the planet. Value still equals low price, but in a Wal-Mart world, there's not much wiggle room for other retailers to play around. It's simply a game of follow the leader—if you can. The price game is one that Trader Joe's wisely chooses not to play, at least not in the usual way. Rather, the chain has created a new value proposition, one that a growing cadre of consumers across the country have adopted wholeheartedly.

The supermarket industry, in general, seems to have a somewhat casual relationship with value, leading many in the industry to believe that most retailers have been inconsistent in their message and commitment to the concept. For the most part, value has been a matter of trying to have the lowest price à la Wal-Mart. Price, most observers agree, is the low-hanging fruit in retailing. On a longer-term basis, however, items and categories become commoditized, and price becomes relatively easy for others to match or beat. In other words, you might have the best value on ground beef and laundry detergent this week, but will you hold onto this position—and the same group of consumers—next week when manufacturer deals change? In fact, most industry research on consumer shopping patterns indicates that consumers are continuing to unbundle their shopping experiences. As a result, no one store, retailer, or even channel owns a category or shopper anymore. Retailers of every stripe are locked in a constant battle to win over consumers, and whatever was done last week doesn't seem to count for much. Consumers ask, "What have you done for me lately?"

"Traditionally, retailers could compete on prices, categories, clean stores, and service. Today, they're working hard to define a unique shopping experience for consumers that cannot be duplicated," notes industry consultant Bill Bishop. "Even though retailers may not own a category, they can own an experience. Creating and replicating an experience through in-store marketing and in-store events is one way of creating a competitive advantage." Even Wal-Mart, the icon of discounting, is reinventing its value proposition by aggressively moving beyond price, working with vendors to create unique in-store events that capture consumers' attention.[2]

"Sharp price points are the cost of entry into this business," adds consultant Gretchen Gogesch. "I'd like to think the entire industry is going beyond price in an effort to become more consumercentric. That's the future."

FOCUS ON THE BRAND

While everyone agrees with this in principle, retailers large and small have let the value proposition slip away because of their focus on a price-only strategy that concentrates primarily on national brands. This seems to have become the natural order of things in retailing ever since Wal-Mart supercenters burst into the collective consciousness of the industry in 1991. Since then, an intense and sometimes bloody battle for the consumer wallet has been fought at the nation's cash registers. By all indications, the battle has not reached its climax. According to a McKinsey & Company report, the majority of regional and national chains has yet to feel the full force of value retailers such as the Wal-Mart supercenters.

While this battle has consumed retailers of every shape and size, often the large chains fail to provide the kind of value that niche players like Trader Joe's offer. Put another way, national and regional chains that can't differentiate themselves from the competition in any given marketplace are far more vulnerable to the massive supercenters than Trader Joe's.

There are several reasons for this vulnerability. First, large companies can't move as quickly to adapt to changes in consumer tastes. Additionally, many publicly held chains vehemently defend their agendas and price strategies in an attempt to feed the financial beast called Wall Street. And any company that becomes totally driven by the bottom line will usually end up destroying entrepreneurial endeavors and wipe out any and all attempts to define value as anything other than price.

Along these lines, McKinsey has identified five imperatives designed to help retailers rethink their business and hone in on real value:[3]

1. *Decide what you're going to be famous for.* Reinvent and define a compelling brand proposition to regain traffic and basket size. This can be done with merchandise assortment, the in-store shopping experience, convenience, or service—anything that helps a retailer stand apart from the competition. A good model to follow is Walgreen's, which has built a superior brand proposition around the authority of its pharmacies, convenience of store locations, vast merchandise assortment, and solid price positioning.

2. *Achieve a lean price structure.* Faced with high costs for good locations and, in many cases, union wage rates, management must mount a war on other costs and rethink the basic operating model so as not to "leave a single penny

on the table." Although this philosophy has been applied primarily at manufacturing firms, many techniques, including pulling rather than pushing merchandise through the system and removing bottlenecks in the supply chain, apply to retailing.

3. *Get credit for value delivered.* It's critical for conventional stores to sharpen pricing on key items that consumers want. The challenge lies in identifying these items and ensuring profitable execution. Retailers should also be rethinking in-store assortment, including using private labels, to guarantee favorable prices and make sure those prices are adequately promoted in the store.

4. *Outexecute the competition through simplification.* Win over consumers through superior in-store execution. This means maintaining consistent in-stock levels, merchandise assortment, and service experiences and responding quickly to changes in the competitive environment. Additionally, driving in-store execution requires more streamlined decision making and eliminating multiple levels of management staffed by people who are not equipped to make optimal decisions. In other words, reduce management layers.

5. *Grow through new categories or formats.* Identify growth opportunities inside and outside the store by using the knowledge of customer behavior and preferences and by continually evaluating both new categories and the competition. Moreover, retailers must also move beyond core formats to grow and adopt a portfolio approach to the business, meaning the development of multiple formats within one company. Value will be created by retailers who move to multiple formats, including small urban stores, convenience stores, traditional supermarkets, and hypermarkets.

OFFER VALUE BEYOND PRICE

Of course, not all large companies are shortsighted or unable to provide value on a timely basis. Many adhere to a value proposition that is not all about dollars and cents. They have redefined value to include quality ingredients and marketplace appeal and have been rewarded by Wall Street for their ability to innovate.

Leading packaged goods companies, which once focused only on price, now see retailers as marketing platforms for their products. One example on the manufacturing side is Procter & Gamble, which has joined the ranks of consumercentric companies working hard to shift to a corporate mind-set that revolves around innovation. On the retail side, Costco's warehouse membership club is a good example of a chain sticking to its value image. "Price is not usually the main issue for shopping here when you talk to customers. It's the experience and the items they offer," Gogesch notes. Clearly, this chain has assembled the ingredients for a shifted value equation that goes beyond price. Here, value has become a matter of quality and product differentiation. "It's a brilliant strategy, and Trader Joe's has done the same thing on a different scale," she says. "There is an overall corporate strategy at work here, an umbrella entity that people recognize. Within that are the subbrands that people love. These take a long time to develop with suppliers and are not just knockoffs of national brands—whether it's low-sodium tomato sauce or chocolate truffles. They are a brilliant hybrid of many different strategies. But it all gets down to offering consumers something beyond what they get at the local supermarket."

For any company, it's become more important than ever to keep an eye on the prize. This means focusing on what will make consumers happy instead of looking at things strictly from a store buyer's point of view. This is a difficult strategy for most chains, because it requires a significant change in mind-set—

from simply being replenishers or restockers to becoming consumer advocates. This may be an overstatement to some, but Trader Joe's success, or that of any retailer, comes from knowing its shoppers and keeping customer satisfaction at the center of everything that's done within the organization. This is truly creating value. "You can't just create a product and then ask on the back end what consumers think of it," says Gogesch. "The process happens the other way around, and true success requires a combination of organizational strategy, consumer opinions, and work with suppliers."

It was interesting to note that on a recent visit to a Trader Joe's store in Oceanside, New York, the tagline beneath the store's name had been changed from *A unique grocery store* to *A grocery store of great values*. This subtlety probably goes unnoticed by the majority of shoppers, but it speaks to the heart of what Trader Joe's is all about.

FOCUS ON VALUE

So what exactly is Trader Joe's value proposition? Taking the broad view, it shows up in almost everything the company does. For one thing, Trader Joe's is the ultimate practitioner of consumercentric behavior. This is a popular and overused term among retailers, most of whom pay only lip service to the concept that the customer comes first. "They [Trader Joe's] don't have a bad quarter and say, 'Screw the values; let's focus on the bottom line,'" observes Gogesch. "They are consistent in staying true to what got them where they are."

Trader Joe's is one of the few retailers that lives and breathes two basic doctrines. Rule number one: The customer is always right. Rule number two: See rule number one.

Another variation of this idea is moving from the Golden Rule to the Platinum Rule.[4] While the Golden Rule says "Do unto others as you would want them to do unto you," the Platinum Rule goes to another level by noting, "Do not do unto others as you would want them to do unto you, because their tastes may not be the same." It goes even further: "Do unto others as others want to be done unto."

Again, this philosophy is not a passing fancy. It is deeply entrenched in the Trader Joe's nature and is the essence of its success. It may sound trite, but this is a company for which delivering value is a social responsibility—something it is compelled to do instead of focusing entirely on the bottom line. However, judging from recent performance, this orientation certainly hasn't hurt the profit and loss statement.

Even for a retailer that does everything right—or tries to—value remains somewhat intangible. "The concept of value in the supermarket industry is about as clear as mud," says Ken Harris of Cannondale Associates. "Is a $2 bottle of wine a value compared to one that costs $390? Yes, but not if it tastes like garbage."

Whatever the product, the value proposition of Trader Joe's lies in its ability to remain extremely focused on what it is and what the company is all about, notes Bill Bishop. "All you have to do is look at their Web site to get an idea of their commitment to quality products at a good price," the consultant observes. "They do a great job of being the buying agent for the consumer. I think we've just given lip service to that in the supermarket industry. But when you actually go out and identify or invent new products, you become an active buying agent. They are very proactive in finding products that deliver unique and significant value. The only time they've violated these principles is in perishables—particularly produce. But it wasn't intentional."

However, perishables like produce and meat are difficult to do right in a store with such a small footprint. Trader Joe's offers these categories because it wants to have a well-rounded product portfolio for customers. But if push came to shove and produce disappeared from Trader Joe's stores, people wouldn't feel cheated. It is simply not an essential part of the chain's value proposition. On the other hand, it would be a mistake for the company to expand its produce offerings and offer subpar products. That would have a negative impact on the chain's value.

Another layer of value springs from the environment and culture that Trader Joe's creates among its customers and employees. Simply, the idea is that shopping can and should be theater—a fun, adventurous experience to which people can look forward, not something they dread. The value proposition is, as previously noted, inherent in the chain's DNA, and it simply wouldn't settle for anything less.

At the same time, price remains an important part of the equation—but not on everything Trader Joe's sells. In fact, the low-price part of the value equation is sometimes more perception than anything else. This perception makes the chain just as difficult to compete with as any other retailer. But the store is really about offering consumers an easy-to-shop environment jammed with products they can't get anywhere else. They don't have to trudge through miles of aisles at the local superstore to get a few pennies off on Tide. Not that Trader Joe's sells Tide or any other national brand.

That's an important part of the chain's value proposition as well. An extensive and unique private label line (as discussed in Chapter 3) keeps Trader Joe's out of the competitive fray. No one else sells Trader José's raspberry salsa or Trader Ming's ginger peanut noodle salad. Therefore, the company can set prices that are attractive to consumers without cutting deeply into the bottom line, the way lowball pricing does at other chains. This is a good competitive landscape to build on.

Additionally, Trader Joe's uses none of the doorbuster sales, double couponing, or buy-one-get-one-free offers so prevalent in the industry at large. As noted, that kind of value is transient and lasts only as long as the sale itself. Many supermarkets have become as much of a commodity as the products on their shelves, attracting an army of cherry pickers who shop the store for deals and nothing else. If Trader Joe's was only about low price, the chain wouldn't be doing as well as it is. The chain certainly appeals to value seekers but specifically to those with higher incomes—usually in the $50,000-plus range, according to figures from ACNielsen.

Low price has no meaning if a product has no economic, practical, or emotional value to customers. Most students of retailing would agree that it is virtually impossible to set a pricing strategy without knowing the value that customers ascribe to goods and services as opposed to the price they are willing to pay. Trader Joe's has mastered a lesson that many others have yet to learn—that retailers and stores are not in business simply to sell more products. They are value delivery systems.

At the center of the chain's value proposition are its people. We'll keep coming back to Trader Joe's people throughout this book. These goodwill ambassadors in Hawaiian shirts make Trader Joe's unique. It goes without saying that they are among the friendliest and most helpful store employees that you are likely to come across in the supermarket industry.

This clearly has a dual purpose. Hiring people who like to engage customers in conversation creates an opportunity to do some suggestive selling. This only works because offering consistent value has enabled Trader Joe's to build an incredible amount of trust with its customers. If a store associate tells you how good an item is or gets you to try something that goes along with it, it's because you trust and value the opinion. Additionally, store employees do a kind of research on the fly to find out what customers like and don't like. If you don't ask, you can't find out what they value. This information, cross-sectioned with sales data and customer comments, which the company really does read, gives Trader Joe's an unusually detailed look at what's moving and allows it to act efficiently on local preferences.

The danger that some observers point out, inherent in any company, is whether the company's consumercentric value strategy will waver as it continues to grow. Concern about the future is natural for any company. But as odd as it may sound, some observers hope that Trader Joe's does not fixate too much on the future and get blindsided by what's going on around it now. They hope it instead takes advantage of opportunities that come up. Juggling present opportunities with future strategies requires great skill. Companies fail when they don't pay attention to what's going on around them and become totally invested in future strategies, forgetting what current customers truly value.

STAY INNOVATIVE

Without question, Trader Joe's preserves current value to customers in a number of ways—not the least of which is sticking to its small store format. This is no accident or a failure to come up with a concept that would fit larger sites. Small stores allow for greater intimacy and more engagement between customers and employees on the selling floor. Part of the value proposition here is simply the size or "shopability" of the store. You have to think of the primary customer of Trader Joe's as the CEO of the household. This is a woman between 21 and 45 years of age who may be pushing a stroller around. Between packing up the car with the kids, making sure she has snacks to keep them placated, and finding a parking space, she's exhausted by the time she gets to the store. Shopability becomes key to her, and organizations that keep an eye on how they design their shopping experiences will come out ahead.

"Look at places like IKEA. They do a brilliant job of providing a shopping experience that women can enjoy and a tremendous price/value equation. The store itself is huge and seemingly overwhelming. But they've broken it down into different pods on each floor to make sure it's more navigable," says Gogesch. "They give you maps to show you where everything is, and there are arrows all over the place pointing to where you might want to go. They also have a childcare area that scores a lot of bonus points with parents. Perhaps most important, and most relevant in terms of what Trader Joe's is doing, is that they offer high style and design at very sharp price points. They don't sacrifice one for the other. In its own way, Trader Joe's does exactly the same thing." As Gogesch notes, it all comes down to treating people with respect and wanting to give them something special, instead of just being a gorilla on price. People are willing to pay a higher price for companies that provide a value-added experience.

Another issue in IKEA's favor, as with Trader Joe's, is that employees are trained to be helpful. Chains like Wal-Mart and conventional retailers across the country are saddled with an army of mostly low-wage, part-time employees who simply don't care. The companies themselves view labor strictly as an expense rather than something that adds value to the shopping trip. People want to be treated with a Neiman Marcus sensibility even if they just have a Kmart budget. The whole idea of giving people more than their budget might allow is inherent in the value proposition for the ever-changing line of Trader Joe's private label products, which have captured an extraordinary share of mind among consumers. This value proposition even applies to the packaging on products, which is presented with far more care than even the largest companies have dared to do. This speaks to the changing definitions of value among consumers. In the recession-ravaged 1970s, value was demonstrated by the black-and-white generic label products whose ubiquitous packaging gave no clue to what was inside. These products had their day. But in the end—something that came rather quickly for generics—consumers realized these products held little value. Trader Joe's not only takes greater care with the presentation of its products but enhances their value by demanding that vendors meet specs on both price and quality.

Interestingly, while the rest of the retail food industry is focusing on stuffing more and more products onto the shelves, Trader Joe's continues to carry a select number of items. This, too, enhances the value proposition according to industry observers, who note that such a focused inventory strategy helps the chain keep costs down while enhancing its ability to be creative in the products that it offers.

CHAPTER 7

Uncover the Right Location

I t's tangible, it's solid, it's beautiful, and it's artistic from my standpoint—I just love real estate." So says television personality, best-selling author, and real estate mogul Donald Trump, whose love affair with commercial and residential developments— while not always wildly profitable—has been well documented. Trader Joe's, unlike The Donald, is not about to wax poetic over the artistry of its latest shopping center lease. The company is more apt to pull out the metaphors for salmon roulette with Florentine stuffing or to tout the joys of real German apple strudel. But real estate in development-friendly cities and towns is becoming an increasingly important issue to the California-based chain as it slowly advances across the country, entering new markets and adding locations in existing ones.

While many retailers are seduced by prime property in high-traffic, popular locations, Trader Joe's has long followed a different path. The company seeks to create an inner beauty of sorts in buildings that often look downright dingy from the outside. That's because Trader Joe's often seeks out abandoned retail space, frequently in out-of-the-way spots where rents are cheap and where both landlords and other tenants are all too happy to see the company move in.

Contrary to what some may believe, there is no shortage of viable and potentially lucrative locations that fit the bill. Real estate industry sources have estimated that 500 million square feet of excess, abandoned, or underdeveloped retail space is sitting out there waiting. Some of that is made up of 6,000- to 200,000-square-foot strip malls, often considered a relic of the 1950s and the subject of a love/hate relationship among developers and tenants. However, many of these are now being redeveloped into community or lifestyle centers to attract higher-quality tenants like Trader Joe's and other less transient clientele. Even some big-box retailers are starting to seek these off-mall locations.

Among the reasons for all this excess space are consolidation and the economic slowdown. For example, Albertsons supermarkets, based in Boise, Idaho, has shed 10 to 20 percent of its stores annually in recent years due either to consolidation or the sale of underperforming units. We're not necessarily talking about bad locations. These are simply sites that may not have penciled out for a particular retailer in terms of customer traffic, sales, or profit per square foot. This creates a terrific opportunity for niche retailers like Trader Joe's, whose operating model is far different from that of larger chains and can draw the traffic needed to make a go of what others might consider a secondary location.

The Trader Joe's model also favors leasing over buying or developing shopping centers on its own. By leasing, the company can use its money to fund and grow operations instead of putting it into land. This is a plus for developers and landlords looking for high-quality tenants that are in business for the long haul. But it's also a strategy that some pundits call a mistake, because land will only continue to increase in price and value over time, and because it is the one commodity you can't make more of. Meanwhile, in an ultracompetitive environment like retailing—specifically grocery retailing—where profits are counted in pennies rather than dollars, real estate has sometimes become a safe haven with a return on investment that can far outstrip selling groceries. As commercial real estate goes, retail has held fairly steady in recent years. It has been virtually recession-resistant, and there's no shortage of capital chasing what's viewed as a safe investment.

But Trader Joe's never intended to be a real estate investment company or landlord. It's a unique niche retailer with a site-selection strategy that combines hard-core demographic analysis, a gut feeling about where future business is going to be, and cheap rent. It sells stuff to people who clamor for what it has, and the company creates a need among those who don't. Then again, there's the old axiom that says there are three factors in successful retailing: "location, location, location."

SEEK OUT SYNERGIES

Officials at Trader Joe's usually decline to discuss any aspect of their operations, preferring products to be in the limelight and operations to be in the background. However, in a 2003 interview with *Shopping Centers Today,* published by the International Council of Shopping Centers in New York, a Trader Joe's spokesman said, "We don't want to be in big shopping centers. We would rather have a freestanding pad or be in a small center with (other) tenants [that are] synergistic with us." Such synergistic retailers may include a Petco, Target, Walgreens, apparel shops, and even supermarkets, the latter rarely competing on the same level as Trader Joe's. For instance, in San Diego, California, a Trader Joe's lies comfortably in the same strip mall as a large Ralph's grocery store.

Doug Yokomizo, Trader Joe's general council and the person responsible for hammering out new lease agreements, was quoted as saying, "We get a lot of calls from a lot of customers, lots of city council members, redevelopment agencies, and other groups clamoring for a Trader Joe's." That's one reason Trader Joe's can set up shop in these out-of-the-way locations. Customers want the store so much, they seek out the company and have no qualms about making a special trip. Few other retailers could succeed at doing business in nonpeak traffic areas, which is why most of the sites Trader Joe's takes over were abandoned by businesses that failed to make them work.

All this pent-up demand has not caused the chain to change its real estate or site-selection strategy. Instead, it has made some minor modifications, such as no longer confining expansion to older strip shopping centers. In all likelihood, the company will continue to avoid mammoth shopping centers, which get plenty of the traffic but aren't really conducive to Trader Joe's goal of being a national chain of neighborhood stores. However, some propitious moves by management have brought stores into moderate-sized community shopping centers in which the rent—although higher than what was paid in the past—is still within corporate parameters. This no doubt pleases parent company Aldi, whose cost-containment strategies—including rent—are legendary. Theo Albrecht, who founded the chain with his brother Karl, was not above turning off lights in offices and stores when he didn't think they were necessary.

In addition to shopping centers in developed suburban areas, the chain is also focusing on urban opportunities and, according to some sources, stands an even better chance of penetrating inner-city markets than Wal-Mart does. Overall, Trader Joe's is adding an average of 15 stores annually, a slow and steady growth rate that enables it to keep debt off the balance sheet and to take advantage of opportunities as they arise. These opportunities are not only in new markets but also in areas that the company is already strong in, yet needs some additional stores to meet consumer demand. As the history of Trader Joe's shows, demand for its presence can travel pretty quickly by word of mouth.

At the same time, the chain is expanding its definition of what constitutes a good site. On one level, this means focusing on, or at least considering, slightly larger stores. Don't expect to see 40,000- to 50,000-square-foot Trader Joe's outlets in the foreseeable future. This size outlet simply wouldn't fit the mold, because a small environment is one of the factors that differentiate the company from the rest of the retail pack. Also, customers would likely rebel at the sight of a big-box Trader Joe's. For the company, smaller is better, and for many longtime shoppers, such a move would be akin to heresy. Besides, new locations, like the 13,000-square-foot unit at the Green Firs Village Shopping Center in the Tacoma, Washington, market are 30 to 40 percent larger than stores opened just a few years ago. In Pasadena, a new 15,000-square-foot store is located on the second level of a 136,000-square-foot mall called The Shops on South Lake Avenue. This is unusual for any grocery store, but it works here because of exclusive parking.[1] It's also another indication that the chain is becoming increasingly flexible in site selection to get a foothold in neighborhoods with the right demographics.

At some point, the search for new types of sites may put Trader Joe's into competition for space with other major retailers. A number of chains, faced with heightened competition from supercenters like Wal-Mart, have jumped on the diversification bandwagon as well. They have begun adding smaller, more manageable units with a specialty store ambiance that also provide busy consumers with more convenient and quicker shopping trips. In smaller locations, parking can be an issue. But turnover in a Trader Joe's store is pretty fast. Parking is evaluated the same way it is for convenience stores—by looking at the number of cars per stall per day. Trader Joe's has down to a science how much time people spend in its stores and what kind of turnover it needs in the parking lot to keep everyone coming in and out efficiently.

Let's be clear. Trader Joe's executives are not abandoning the search for smaller 9,000- to 10,000-square-foot sites. This is still the kind of space available for anchor stores in older or re-furbished strip malls. It's also the type of structure that allows the company to know exactly what it can generate in terms of sales per square foot—a figure that Trader Joe's generally posts at twice the industry average. Location and small space have been points of differentiation for Trader Joe's since the begin-ning. It's a brilliant strategy that is the diametric opposite of the typical retail chain mentality, which is to steer clear of B and C locations. However, Trader Joe's has something few large chains have—rabid customer loyalty. This gives the company some-thing no big-box retailer can buy at any price—passionate word of mouth.

FIND BEAUTIFUL SHELLS

In discussing the company's real estate strategy, consultant Kevin Kelley says, "Trader Joe's finds a shell at the bottom of the ocean that no one else wants and makes it work. Most su-permarkets would never think of putting a store in a center that has another grocery store, deli, or bagel shop. But Trader Joe's likes them because those stores draw traffic, and they know people will still come to them for unique items."

The chain's interest in secondary locations has also gained it the loyalty of those real estate experts across the country who handle these properties. They usually have to deal with nail sa-lons, hobby shops, tattoo parlors, and a plethora of other local businesses that can close as quickly as they open. Trader Joe's, on the other hand, is a proven, hot concept that wants to come into their space, pays its rent on time, and increases customer traffic to the center. What real estate agent, landlord, or devel-oper wouldn't be grateful to have old real estate recycled by a top-notch company. As a sweetener, they're happy to offer Trader Joe's a great lease rate.

On the other hand, this company does not ignore opportunities that arise in choice areas because of any quasireligious belief that you can only operate successfully in a certain size store in a specific location. The company knows from experience that a slightly larger store will work without losing the informal, homey style that Trader Joe's aficionados would sorely miss. Additionally, larger stores offer greater flexibility in merchandising—particularly in perishables—yet can still be small enough to use in urban areas like New York City, Chicago, or downtown San Francisco.

The expansion program for Trader Joe's really began in 1991, when former CEO John Shields became concerned that keeping the chain strictly on the West Coast would be too limiting in the long run. Even now, the company continues to grow slowly, taking its time finding just the right locations. It's a good strategy, according to Kelly. "The number one enemy of any organization is growth that takes place too quickly," he insists. "There is little danger of this happening [to Trader Joe's] unless one or more of several things transpire: Trader Joe's goes public and starts to get pushed by shareholders and Wall Street analysts, Aldi changes its longtime hands-off policy, or Trader Joe's borrows to the hilt instead of financing new stores from internal cash flow." All of these scenarios are highly unlikely. Yet one thing is eminently clear: the chain is moving into new markets and taking advantage of locations that fit its unique format.

Parent company Aldi is much like Trader Joe's when it comes to setting limits on what it pays for rental space. But Aldi is far more rigid in the way it goes about building. Trader Joe's is obviously willing to take over someone else's location and is flexible when it comes to the size and shape of the structure. It doesn't care whether the building is square or oblong, as long as it gets it into the market it wants at the right price. But Aldi has a build-to-suit strategy and prefers to do its construction from the ground up. "If Aldi wants a 10,158-square-foot box, then by God that's what they're going to build," according to one industry observer.

MAKE IT THERE, MAKE IT ANYWHERE

One of the most anticipated real estate strategies is how Trader Joe's will fare in taking on Manhattan with its 9,000- to 12,000-square-foot sites. As the song says, "If you can make it there, you'll make it anywhere." The company has long operated stores in outlying suburbs like Long Island and in affluent areas of Westchester County. But it is biding its time in taking a bite out of the Big Apple. As lucrative as the New York City market may be, it can be a dismal failure for the best operators. Rental space is expensive, and you have to rely on foot traffic in a city that has one or more food stores of different persuasions on every block.

As every retailer knows, massive urban renewal means that the inner city can no longer be ignored. Of course, suburban growth will continue, although the suburban sprawl that characterized the last several decades may be coming to an end in mature markets. Smart growth for Trader Joe's will increasingly take advantage of opportunities in urban areas, which house residents that spend an estimated $85 billion on retail products annually. That number will continue to grow exponentially along with the population over the next 20 years. Much of this new population will gravitate toward reclaimed urban areas near transit lines. This density of population makes areas like New York City far more attractive to retailers like Trader Joe's than a place like Malibu, California, which certainly has an upscale customer base but not the density of population needed to support such a store.

Interestingly, Trader Joe's may, for the first time, find itself competing for sites with some big-box retailers for whom Manhattan seems to be the new hot button. Home Depot's three-story home improvement center was opened with considerable fanfare, and retailers like Costco, Wal-Mart, and Target are said to be scouting potential "vertical" sites as well. Whole Foods, the closest rival to Trader Joe's, now has two stores on the island, one in the redeveloped Chelsea neighborhood on Manhattan's West Side. This is also one of the areas in which Trader Joe's is interested. At press time, Trader Joe's was closing the deal for a 15,000 square foot store in New York City's busy and trendy Union Square neighborhood in a building that also houses a New York University dormitory. Whole Foods also has a large store in Union Square.

A relatively new technology, cart escalators, makes it easier for big-box retailers to go vertical and enter locations they wouldn't have gone after in the past. Theoretically, you can move a Wal-Mart into a four-story building on the East Side of New York or other spaces that would not have been feasible before. The only problem with going vertical is that there's no room for parking. You therefore need a huge customer base within walking distance to make these locations work. This is less of an issue for Trader Joe's than for 100,000-square-foot stores with a different profit model. Besides, if anyone fits Trader Joe's customer profile, it's the typical urban customer—overeducated, underpaid, and still willing to spend $15 or $20 on a bottle of wine or fork over a few dollars to try a new type of raspberry salsa or vegetarian pizza.

"Trader Joe's is considering opening multiple locations in Manhattan," according to Robert Futterman, CEO of Robert K. Futterman & Associates, which has been retained by the chain to search out viable locations. "We have conducted extensive market analysis to determine appropriate sites and have already toured a number of them. The ideal locations are in Manhattan's high-density residential neighborhoods." Another potential plus is that New York stores rely on walk-in business. Trader Joe's, however, is used to operating stores with parking lots, which take up a lot of space. Therefore, a store with the right demographic in the Big Apple, with customers who walk in on foot, could potentially produce sales twice that of any other in the chain's roster.

This seems to be underscored by figures from ACNielsen indicating that urban shoppers are just the ticket. According to ACNielsen, six out of ten Trader Joe's shoppers have annual incomes of $50,000-plus. Furthermore, dominant characteristics of the average Trader Joe's customer speak to an urban lifestyle. These include the following:

- Childless younger couples
- Young singles
- Middle-aged singles
- Middle-aged childless couples

MODIFY FOR NEW MARKETS

At present, Trader Joe's is not changing its real estate strategy so much as modifying it. No doubt the company will push into major metro markets as it is trying to do in New York and has already successfully done in Chicago and San Francisco. Of course, size is a factor, but Trader Joe's has been able to penetrate inner cities better than Wal-Mart has, because its target audience is urban consumers looking for a value proposition.

This isn't to say there aren't issues to overcome if you want to stay on friendly terms with everyone when doing business in a big city. This was the case with an 11,000-square-foot store with two levels of parking on Market Street in San Francisco's Castro district. Trader Joe's already had a store on Geary Street near the Presidio but still had to convince residents of the Castro that the store would fit into the neighborhood and not disrupt traffic and parking. The latter was in very short supply, and community activists were not immediately impressed with a plan by

Trader Joe's to build 48 parking spots. At its other store in the city, the company had to hire security guards just to keep traffic moving.

Problems with the locals are usually reserved for big-box retailers like Wal-Mart, which seems to be in a constant battle with residents, zoning boards, and other local bureaucracies trying to keep the company out. It's the classic NIMBY syndrome—Not In My Back Yard. When Trader Joe's scouts for new locations, the locals—many of whom already know the chain—are waiting with open arms and wallets. In fact, local activists who usually oppose new developments often go on letter-writing campaigns, trying to get the company to come to their neighborhood. The Trammell Crow Company, one of the country's largest commercial landlords and developers, was inundated with letters of support when a proposed Trader Joe's site in Washington's upscale Georgetown neighborhood was in danger of being quashed by the area's Historic Preservation Review Board.

As testament to what a good tenant the company is, in a 2004 survey by the International Council of Shopping Centers that asked landlords and developers which retailers they would prefer to have in their centers, Trader Joe's was among the top five—and it was the only food store on the list. Other retailers included H&M, the Swedish clothing retailer; Build-A-Bear Workshop; teen clothiers Hollister and Hot Topic; and Victoria's Secret.

Despite the current interest in urban markets, Trader Joe's is certainly not abandoning its bread and butter—smaller, somewhat outdated strip shopping centers that first started dotting America's suburban landscape in the 1940s. Many of these locations are not what they once were—they're better. Some observers call these sites a relic of the 1950s, when they became popular in burgeoning post–World War II suburbia. Their popularity continued into the 1960s, when they fell out of favor with retailers looking for larger sites with more parking to accommodate increasingly mobile consumers. General merchandise retailers and department stores then headed for newly minted enclosed malls, while many supermarket chains started building or leasing larger freestanding sites.

Many of the era's strip centers simply fell out of favor and into disrepair, and landlords and developers had little incentive to do anything about it. One reason is that small stores—ranging from beauty shops and tattoo parlors to 99-cent outlets and dry cleaners—took over the space. Some were solid local businesses, but others were underfinanced and closed up as quickly as they opened.

However, the tide has turned and strip centers—often considered dead space—are in demand and making a comeback in a kind of suburban renewal. For one thing, the mall experience is wearing thin for many who are unwilling to make time-consuming visits to these megacenters. Smaller stores are also abandoning mall locations because of lower traffic, escalating rents, and competition from chain retailers. Wal-Mart is not just a grocery retailer. It is a formidable competitor in electronics, shoes, jewelry, furniture, pharmaceuticals, stationery, and photofinishing—businesses that are often the first victims when a supercenter like Wal-Mart takes over a mall location.[2]

FLAUNT YOUR STABILITY

In some respects, the real estate strategy employed by Trader Joe's has long been ahead of the curve in concentrating on those neighborhood shopping centers that are usually located on main streets between well-developed residential areas. This provides the stores with enough population density to develop a strong sales base, yet they're located in older and cheaper centers that are often too small to attract large anchor tenants like supermarkets or drugstores. Supermarkets and other food stores have always been preferred tenants among landlords and developers, who feel they bring in traffic and are usually willing to sign long-term leases. Because of this, supermarkets have traditionally paid the lowest rents in any development.

This was certainly true during the 2000–2001 recession, when regional shopping centers (or "power centers") were in trouble and supermarkets and drugstores kept occupancy stable. Trader Joe's used this fact to its advantage to gain long-term leases for some very reasonable prices—$15 per square foot or less—along with other lucrative concessions.

Trader Joe's may continue to have the pick of the litter when it comes to these locations. However, it should be noted that, at this writing, favorable financing and interest rates have sent landlords into a frenzy of renovating centers, some of which are more than 30 years old. The reason, of course, is to attract well-known tenants with favorable lease rates. Once an older neighborhood center is renovated, lease rates can escalate 20 to 40 percent. As such, some real estate industry observers say that Trader Joe's may not find as many sites in the future as it once did for the same prices it's used to paying.

Other industry observers note that Trader Joe's often takes over deserted locations in old strip centers where landlords are more than happy to lower the rent, especially for a higher-quality tenant that can drive traffic to the site. As such, the rent factor has to be an impressive part of the chain's balance sheet. In fact, $15 per square foot may not be unusual. Some locations cost the chain as little as $10 per square foot, with landlords making up the shortfall on nonanchor stores.

"I have no doubt they've negotiated some good deals and have been pretty successful with their real estate," says Scott Muldavin, president of The Muldavin Company, a real estate developer and investment firm in San Raphael, California. "In general, the real difficulty in food retailing is protecting against Wal-Mart. So, while the mainstream supermarket chains battle each other and Wal-Mart, Trader Joe's has been able to step out of the traditional grocery-anchored retail center and focus on smaller spaces that others don't want."

As noted, Trader Joe's represents a stable tenant among a volatile group of small ones, like dry cleaners and video stores. In effect, Trader Joe's becomes a strong anchor for these small shopping centers and draws other higher-quality retailers to the same sites. "They have strong financials and would be a good catch for any landlord," Muldavin adds. Even if the company finds itself competing a bit more for the best sites, cost may not be an issue. The company can afford to pay more if it has to, especially in locations that carry more high-margin products like wine. Normally, real estate accounts for approximately 10 percent of a company's operating expenses. Paying an extra $3 per square foot to get a good location is no big deal if it means you're going to sell more products.

Recently, Trader Joe's has expanded its real estate horizons. In addition to urban locations and searching for secondary or B locations in old strip centers, stores are now being opened in midrange community shopping centers of 300,000 or 400,000 square feet, locations that might even be home to a small Wal-Mart or another discounter. One example is the Emeryville, California, location. Once a largely industrial area, this city at the foot of San Francisco's Bay Bridge is now home to a diverse up-and-coming population, and it's home to a number of high-tech firms such as Pixar Animation Studios. The mall there has been highly successful, featuring several clothing stores, a sporting goods retailer, and others. Trader Joe's sits on an outparcel of the parking lot. It's been a big draw for the center and a hugely successful store for the company.

Another great location is in Chicago's Lincoln Park neighborhood, which one industry analyst calls the "epicenter" for Trader Joe's. It has people with education, affluence, and density of population—everything the chain could possibly hope for. The company did have to take a second-floor location in this strip development and, even though there's a parking garage, access is not ideal. It's a classic example of real estate parameters preventing Trader Joe's from paying for a ground floor location.

Some analysts feel this move may turn out to be a mistake, saying the company is missing out on the ability to maximize sales in this location by being wedded to a low-cost real estate strategy. In Lincoln Park, Trader Joe's might have had to pay $30 to $35 per square foot to get the ground floor space, as opposed to the usual $10 to $15. But, by doing so, it may have been able to double the store's sales. Still, looking for more inexpensive space is a formula that works for the company and one to which it is committed. "It's been to their advantage not to pay for 'Main and Main,' and the concept is certainly a destination. Therefore, convenience is not as critical a factor to them as it is to the traditional grocery store," says Neil Stern of McMillan/Doolittle in Chicago. However, it is likely that Trader Joe's will move into more prime locations in the future. Interestingly, it looks as though the company is following the same path as Costco warehouse club stores, which started out taking secondary locations and eventually moved to primary sites. Costco paid more but also got more volume out of those stores.

The old adage, "You get what you pay for," may eventually apply to Trader Joe's real estate endeavors, as it does to most other things in business and life.

CHAPTER 8

Constantly Innovate

T
he rolling, green hills of Northern California's scenic wine country don't look like a cradle of revolution. But that's exactly what they've been in recent years, thanks to a little item affectionately known as Two-Buck Chuck, a line of "extreme value" wines available in most Trader Joe's locations for just $1.99 a bottle. The wines have appeal for customers with even the most discriminating tastes and have both transformed and appalled the staid and snobbish West Coast wine industry.

Over the past several years, the Charles Shaw label has become the stuff of urban legend. One story has it that Trader Joe's purchased a huge batch of wine at closeout prices from an airline that could no longer have corkscrews on board after the September 11 terrorist attacks. Then there's the tale about Charles Shaw being a reclusive billionaire wine lover who created an inexpensive product to introduce American consumers to the joys of wine.

In reality, this bargain-basement bottle is the result of overplanting in the 1990s, which led to a surplus of grapes and wine. Thanks to some creativity, a constant desire for innovation, and a little luck, Trader Joe's used this oversupply to help create the fastest-growing wine label in history, with more than ten million cases of Charles Shaw varietals—Merlot, Shiraz, Chardonnay, Sauvignon Blanc, and Cabernet Sauvignon—sold in just three years.

Aficionados have actually referred to them as flavors rather than varietals, preferring not to dignify a $2 wine. But at one point Trader Joe's stores were selling 1 million cases a month from pallets stacked on the floor near the entrance. It may be the first time in the history of food retailing that wine—and a relatively obscure one at that—was used as a loss leader.

The story of how Trader Joe's achieved this success is a great example of how the company does business. It has built its reputation—and significant profits—by exploiting niches in every category, and in creating markets that people never thought could exist before. Wine, which is a product the company has specialized in from its founding, is no exception.

USE WORD OF MOUTH

The popularity of Charles Shaw wine was based almost solely on word of mouth, which spread like a California wildfire beginning in 2002. Some of it came from wine connoisseurs, who dubbed Two-Buck Chuck not only drinkable but "not bad"— high praise from people whose palates were used to more expensive nectars. Moreover, the products have received international publicity, and some varieties have made a strong showing at wine competitions across the country. This includes the International Eastern Wine Competition in Corning, New York, where Charles Shaw's 2002 California Shiraz was up against some 2,300 wines and walked away with double gold. In 2004, judges gave Charles Shaw's Chardonnay a bronze medal.

The label is sold exclusively in Trader Joe's stores through an arrangement with the Bronco Wine Company in California. It's carried in all stores in California, Arizona, Illinois, Indiana, Michigan, Nevada, Ohio, Oregon, Virginia, and Washington

State, along with selected stores in Massachusetts and New Jersey. The only reason it's not available chainwide is that some state and local laws, like in New York, prohibit the sale of wine in supermarkets—the only time Trader Joe's is defined that way. While the famous $1.99 price is available on the West Coast, the wines actually sell for $3.39 in Ohio as a result of higher distribution costs. Other than that, the price hasn't gone up a penny since being introduced.

Consumers first tried Two-Buck Chuck in 2001 primarily out of curiosity. This adventurous group included oenophiles as well as those used to buying wine in a box or with screw-top caps. Since then, they've been flocking to Trader Joe's stores, not to buy bottles but to haul off cases of the stuff, despite protests from some in the wine community that the inexpensive product is little more than fruit juice and alcohol—a "super juice." Like Trader Joe's itself, Charles Shaw wine, with the help of a little subtle promotion, gained an early cult following in Southern California that rapidly spread to other states.

Take the Emeryville, California, store where people heard through the grapevine that a new shipment of Merlot was arriving. Customers lined up at dawn in anticipation. When the doors finally opened, an entire trailer load of the wine was sold out in a little more than half an hour. This kind of publicity seems to feed on itself and has given rise to other stories about customers backing their Chevy Suburbans up to Trader Joe's loading dock to haul away a big supply of their favorite variety. In return, the buzz created from the Charles Shaw wines brought in a lot of customers who had never shopped at Trader Joe's before or were only occasional visitors but now frequent the stores regularly.

IT DOESN'T HAVE TO BE GREAT IF IT'S CHEAP

Is it a great wine? Well, some wine industry experts feel that it's nothing more than jug wine disguised in a nice bottle with a cork and a taste that's somewhere between weeds and green peppers. Perhaps this is just a case of sour grapes, considering the results of blind taste tests at various competitions where judges were left mumbling about how their careers were going to be ruined after giving Chuck some rave reviews. Some trendy West Coast high schoolers—who aren't supposed to be drinking anyway—have taken to calling it "Up-Chuck." But Charles Shaw wine is exactly what Trader Joe's wants it to be—a great value and an item that keeps customers coming back for more . . . and more. It also goes along with Trader Joe's overall merchandising philosophy, which calls for putting the fun back into shopping and taking the mystery out of food and wine.

Of course, Napa Valley vintners, not exactly renowned for their sense of humor, are less than amused by its success. Competitors fervently deny that the quality of Two-Buck Chuck is anywhere near what they sell and maintain it's certainly not cutting into sales of the region's premium wines. However, they concede that people who have been exposed to $2 wines now expect to find cheap wine all over the place—an apparent case of lowered expectations.

Indeed, because of the success of the Charles Shaw label, cheap wine has become trendy. Most supermarkets and other beverage stores now stock their own brand of $1.99 wine, knowing that smart shoppers will go get it at Trader Joe's if they don't offer an inexpensive version of their own.

BE CAREFUL ABOUT WHAT YOU PUT YOUR NAME ON

So just who is this mysterious Charles Shaw?

Charles F. Shaw—the man, not the label—is a graduate of the Stanford School of Business and an investment banker who bought a Napa Valley Winery with his wife, Lucy, to produce Beaujolais in 1974. That plan, however, didn't work out. When the Shaws went through a messy divorce in 1991, his wife re-portedly ended up with the vineyard, which subsequently went bankrupt. The winery and name were then sold in 1995 to the Bronco Wine Company, run by industry veteran Fred Franzia, for the princely sum of $18,000. It turned out to be an amazing investment, with Charles Shaw wines yielding an impressive $150 million sales by 2003.[1]

Charles Shaw—the man himself—moved to Chicago after the divorce and is involved in the computer software business. He's long been very protective of his reputation in the Napa Valley and his strong relationships with other vintners in that close-knit community. Shaw reportedly has always resented the fact that his name was being used for this cheap, mass-market product. In an interview with ABC News, Shaw said he was upset by the fact that a $2 bottle of wine with his name on it forced his friends in the industry to suffer losses, layoffs, and even clo-sures of some facilities. "I just want my vintner friends in Napa Valley to know that I didn't sell this name to these folks," he said.

As any good news organization would do, ABC went to Fred Franzia and asked what he had to say about this. His reply? "I don't have to say anything. I own it!"

The truth is, California vintners aren't as much upset with the $2 price tag or the Shaw name as they are with Franzia for trying to pass it off as having a Napa Valley origin. The label reads "cellared and bottled in Napa." This is technically true, because Bronco has a huge winery in an industrial area of Napa County and a permit that enables it to bottle as much wine as every other winery in the Napa Valley combined. But it was felt that the label was somewhat misleading, because the wine wasn't made from Napa-grown grapes. Four years ago, area vintners sued to get the word Napa removed from the label. The Cali-fornia Supreme Court ultimately ruled against Franzia in mid-2004. However, those who know the tenacious vintner do not expect him to take the ruling lying down.

On the other hand, not everyone is so negative about the impact of Two-Buck Chuck. Some industry observers feel it's been something of a boon to the industry at large, because it got people talking about wine instead of beer, soda, and coffee—all of which have far greater advertising budgets to throw around.

Aside from the cheap screw-cap brands of the 1970s and a brief flirtation with wine coolers, the United States has never been a mass wine-consuming country—drinking less than three gallons of wine per capita annually. It is simply not the beverage we grew up with, unlike for Europeans. While this relative rarity has given wine a certain snob appeal over the years, it has also kept away consumers who felt that choosing the right wine was simply more trouble than it was worth and who cracked open a familiar bottle of beer instead. The simplicity of the Charles Shaw selection and its low price—not to mention people's innate trust in Trader Joe's to choose a quality product—made it okay just to pick up a bottle without the fear of making a wine faux pas. Even if you hated it, the price was so low you could just throw it away. What is still unclear from all the statistics is whether Two-Buck Chuck brought new wine consumers into the fold or just diluted the purchases of existing drinkers.

Mainstream supermarket chains are now taking advantage of the phenomenal success of Two-Buck Chuck and the consumer's new appreciation of inexpensive wines by hawking their own inexpensive labels. Among them: Wal-Mart's Alcott Ridge; Raley's Cal-Arbor; Safeway's Diablo Creek; and Albertsons's Origins, Jenica Peak Coastal, and Q Sonoma County.

GET THEM TO TRADE UP

Additionally, wine industry observers feel that once the masses get a taste of Chuck, they will eventually trade up to other relatively inexpensive but higher-quality wines in the $7 to $15 range. This may already be happening in California where the Charles Shaw products, albeit still popular, are losing some of the panache—and sales—they had several years ago. Poking holes in that theory is the fact that sales are continuing to grow in Trader Joe's stores outside the West Coast.

Astonishingly, the Charles Shaw label accounted for about 13 percent of table wine sales in California for the first 6 months of 2004. This is a huge number for a gigantic market like the Golden State, which has some 1,200 wineries competing for market share. But there are mixed signals on which way the tide is turning. That number represents a decline of four share points from the same period a year earlier. Total shipments of the product were off 8 percent in the first six months of 2004. This reflects a decline of 28 percent in shipments within California but an increase of 22 percent in shipments to other states, according to Jon Fredrikson, a principal with Gomberg, Fredrickson & Associates in Woodside, California.

Regardless of these short-term blips, Trader Joe's is clearly in wine retailing for the long haul. It's good for profits and image. Two-Buck Chuck is a recent phenomenon, but Trader Joe's carries other labels and has been selling wine for nearly four decades. The company is constantly innovating in this area, introducing new varieties at fair prices and encouraging customers to keep coming to find out what's new.

SELL WHAT YOU LOVE

The company's love affair with wine began in the late 1960s, when founder Joe Coulombe converted the Pronto convenience stores in Pasadena to Trader Joe's to compete with 7-Eleven. Coulombe was selling gourmet foods, including cheeses, which were manufacturer overstocks or closeouts—items that people weren't familiar with anyway. It didn't take long for him to conclude that where you have cheese, you should also have wine.

Back in the late 1960s and early 1970s, most people were drinking mass-market brands like Gallo, Almaden, and Paul Masson. Coulombe decided to make a risky move by buying up mass quantities of European wines from financially strapped vintners and distributors and blowing them out the door at $2 to $3 a bottle. He promoted them through write-ups in the *Fearless Flyer*.

Even after selling Trader Joe's to the Aldi family in Germany, he never really left the wine business. Coulombe, who says he's probably tasted over 100,000 wines in his lifetime, maintains his own Web site to discuss wines and the wine regions he frequently visits. Under his "nom de vin"—http://www.winejoe.com—Coulombe notes that most of the products he's tasted over time have not been terrific. "On the other hand, most samples were submitted by vintners who were desperate for money. That's how Trader Joe's got those low prices. That's also how I learned that a lot of wines that are marginal can be very good—if they are served with the right food."[2]

Coulombe continues to discuss wine in the same consumer-friendly manner he did with all the other products he bought and promoted during his years at Trader Joe's. Rather than trying merely to "sell" a product, he prefers to educate people on the history of winemaking and share information he's picked up in his extensive travels—including two trips a year to the wine regions of Europe. In recent dissertations, he's discussed the wines of the Czech Republic and Tasmania. But he doesn't just talk about the wine. He also discusses the food he was exposed to in the country and how it was served with the wine.

The site is not for the uninitiated. It's as far from the simplistic Two-Buck Chuck as you can get. Coulombe peppers his commentary and descriptions with such folksy phrases as:

- Quite oakey and forward
- Not overtly Burgundian
- A more aggressive character

- Serious but sort of thin
- A very clean juice

Just before Two-Buck Chuck hit the shelves at Trader Joe's in 2000, Coulombe spent a week in Paris on the Left Bank. The objective, as he explained in his electronic newsletter, was "to dine at every restaurant and café mentioned by Ernest Hemingway in *The Sun Also Rises* and *A Moveable Feast*." Incidentally, Coulombe didn't comment on his thoughts about Two-Buck Chuck, and it's still unknown exactly how he feels about the product. To date, he has yet to review any Charles Shaw wines on his site.

STICK TO WHAT YOU KNOW BEST

Fred Franzia, by contrast, shuns the mystique and snobbery associated with wines. That may be because he and his family know more about the nuts and bolts of the wine business than virtually anyone around. Franzia, a distant relative of the Gallo family, owns more than 30 square miles of California vineyards[3] and thinks nothing of taking on the snobbier elements of Napa Valley's wine establishment. The estimated 35,000 acres of vineyards owned by the Bronco Wine Company also produce products under the Forest Glen, Estrella, Montpellier, Grand Cru, Silver Ridge, Hacienda, FoxHollow, and Napa Ridge brands, all inexpensive brands offered by various retailers. The company is also a custom bottler for several national wineries. Last year, the company processed some 300,000 tons of grapes and produced approximately 20 million cases of wine. However, the Franzia name might be most recognized by cash-strapped college students as the original creator of wine in a box.

Franzia's pedigree is as good as that of anyone in the wine business and better than most—especially the amateurs who descended on Northern California's grape-growing region in the 1990s with dreams of making a fortune by opening a bed-and-breakfast and putting in a few vines to cash in on Napa's newfound panache. Come to think of it, the scenario was not unlike that of 150 years earlier, when people with little or no background in prospecting descended on the goldfields of California seeking to make a killing with limited resources.

Franzia is a third-generation winemaker. His grandfather, Guiseppe, came to America from Genoa, Italy, in 1893 and traveled to the Stockton, California, area to begin farming. In 1906, he purchased 80 acres near Ripon, California. A number of years later, Guiseppe was visiting Genoa when his five sons decided the family should get into commercial wine production. They had a facility half completed by the time their father returned.[4]

Production began in 1915 and remained in the family until 1973, when the Coca-Cola Bottling Company of New York purchased the winery. The Franzia brothers, Fred and Joseph, along with their cousin, John, decided to strike out on their own. They formed the Bronco Wine Company in December 1973 in Ceres, California, with some financial backing from Getty Oil. The name is said to be taken from the football team at Santa Clara University where Joseph and Fred went to school.

The Franzias are the first to admit that the business grew faster than they ever thought it would. Today, in addition to being one of the largest wine grape growers in California, the company produces a family of brands that is sold in over 65 countries. To support this volume, Bronco has more than 100 million gallons of steel storage tanks and 80,000 oak barrels in four wineries—located in Ceres, Napa, Sonoma, and Escalon.

Bronco first connected with Trader Joe's in 2000, when the Franzias met with chain executives, including CEO Dan Bane, to discuss creating a wine that would sell for under $2 a bottle. Trader Joe's clearly saw a potential opportunity, and Charles Shaw hit the shelves in 2002 with sales of two million cases the first year.

TIMING IS EVERYTHING

The idea might not have gotten off the ground in the first place had it not been for fortuitous timing. Urban myths aside, overplanting in the 1990s—when the economy was strong, dot-coms had yet to blow up, and everyone was spending like the party would never end—had resulted in a massive glut of wine grapes in California.

When the economy headed south in 2000 and everyone's 401(k) got clobbered virtually overnight, so did the price of grapes, to the point where some growers couldn't scrape enough money together to pay their property taxes. Winemakers prefer to use the word *surplus* when discussing this period. *Glut* sounds too much like *glug* or *chug*, neither of which suits the industry's sensibilities. To wine insiders, the surplus was simply something that was cyclical. Besides, they argued, there's always more supply than demand when it comes to grapes. Overall, the situation wasn't much different than the surpluses of the early 1980s. The yield for the 2000 crop was particularly high, and the overall quality wasn't that great.

Despite the economic turmoil, people still wanted to drink wine. But they also needed to economize, given their shrinking portfolios and incomes. Franzia cashed in on the trend by going downscale. His new product had an upscale-looking label and a cork—albeit synthetic—in a real wine bottle that made people feel like they still had the bucks to spend on life's little indulgences.

Moreover, the wine got great press coverage, giving people the impression they weren't buying cheap wine but rather something that was a great value. As wine columnist Mike Steinberger reported, "The media seem to have an unquenchable thirst for stories that somehow cast doubt on the worthiness of expensive wines and the wisdom of those who drink them. The subtext of many of the articles about Two-Buck Chuck is that the swill-guzzling masses have once again outfoxed the snobs by finding a wine that offers both value and quality."[5]

The truth is somewhere in between. Two-Buck Chuck is a bit of an anomaly in that it's a cheap wine that has a kind of up-scale panache. But it's not the first inexpensive wine to hit the market, and considering recent trends, it certainly won't be the last. The question is whether it has staying power.

"It's never been done quite like this before," says noted wine industry consultant Jon Fredrikson. Fredrikson's firm specializes in winery and vineyard acquisitions and divestitures, along with wine industry economic and marketing analysis. "Two-Buck Chuck came about because of unusual circumstances related to the structure of the market. There are always wines that sell for $1.99 because they end up as closeouts in bins or as distressed goods like dented cans. However, no one bought them and certainly not in quantity. And there have always been cheap imports from Eastern Europe that hit $1.99. But they were just crappy wines and never had a long run."

In this case, however, a giant grower was loaded down with grapes, wine, and a huge production capacity in terms of tanks and bottling facilities. Adding interest and some complications to the story, a Bronco affiliate, Classic Wines of California, is one of the state's largest distributors with an enormous operation of around 200 people selling wines directly for Bronco. Furthermore, Classic Wines has its own trucking fleet, warehouses, and the ability to service customers in-house, thus significantly lowering distribution costs.

Charles Shaw is one label among dozens that the Franzias have purchased over the years at distress sales for little or nothing. However, this deal was particularly attractive for Trader Joe's, because Bronco's operation enabled it to ship directly from production facilities to the chain's warehouse, skipping the middleman and sales organization and, therefore, keeping the raw cost of the product very low. As noted, this is how Trader Joe's prefers to do business.

QUALITY MUST ACCOMPANY PRICE

It's important to emphasize that the success of Two-Buck Chuck was not based on price alone. It also had to do with the relative high quality of the product, compared to other products in the same price range. When Bronco began offering the Shaw label to Trader Joe's, some other excellent wines were available in the bulk market at bargain prices. "I know one instance where a fine winery in the Napa Valley was giving away tanks of Chardonnay, but there was no buyer," Fredrikson shares. "They wanted to clear out their tanks before the 2001 vintage, so they just gifted wine that couldn't find a home."

Franzia was able to obtain some fine coastal wines and blend them into his own surpluses. As such, the initial batches of Charles Shaw were the world's best wine value at the time, according to many observers. "It just knocked everyone's socks off," Fredrickson adds. "My wife first saw it and brought it home. We had our friends over and did some tastings. Everyone went crazy and ran down there to buy cases of the stuff, because they thought it was a one-shot deal on closeouts."

However, as word about Charles Shaw spread, the wines kept coming, and a cult following developed. This was helped along when one Trader Joe's store manager came up with the nickname Two-Buck Chuck. "People don't always remember labels, but they remember Two-Buck Chuck, because we rarely have had nicknames like that come up in the wine industry," Fredrikson observes.

Before long, the product put an enormous dent in the California wine market and, at its peak, accounted for about 20 percent of wine sales in the state. In a category that has always depended on snob appeal, this was exactly the opposite, and people stocked up. "I had a friend who was a real estate broker who showed a lot of high-priced houses in places like Atherton, Woodside, and Palo Alto," Fredrickson says. "She would go into their wine cellars, and there was Charles Shaw. And if you looked around in places like Woodside on recycling day, all you would see were empty bottles of Charles Shaw wine."

The product certainly wasn't being compared with $50 or $60 bottles of wine. But initial batches of the varietals were so good that people couldn't tell the difference between Charles Shaw and a $10 or $15 bottle of wine. All of a sudden, it became fashionable to bring Two-Buck Chuck to even the fanciest dinner party.

Sales seem to have peaked in California in December 2002 at about 600,000 cases a month. But cases have since started to ship regularly to Trader Joe's stores in other states, so sales continue to climb. "Younger people without a lot of money are still buying Charles Shaw, and there are still huge stacks of it in Trader Joe's," Fredrikson notes. "But I think interest has peaked and it's not so much the in thing to do."

Nonetheless, the success of Charles Shaw should be put into perspective, especially because shipments have reached one million cases a month. The *Wine Market Report* estimates that six million cases were sold by the end of 2003, nearly surpassing long-established brands like Beringer and Kendall Jackson. Furthermore, of the estimated 6,500 brands sold in the United States, only a handful has sales of more than one million cases annually.

UPDATE YOUR IMAGE

But there are larger elements at play. Due to imports from Australia and South America, the entire California wine industry has undergone a shakeout. This has reawakened consumer interest in value products, resulting in a whole new value segment—albeit at higher prices than Two-Buck Chuck. As a consequence, a whole host of products in the $4.99 and $5.99 price range is selling like crazy. In essence, Charles Shaw has suffered the same fate that has befallen others in the wine industry—namely that once you're discovered, your image can get somewhat tired and work against you. People have discovered a difference between Charles Shaw and higher-priced products and have traded up.

As painful as this situation has been to mainstream California brands, the popularity of Two-Buck Chuck, along with the influx of Australian labels like Yellowtail and Lindeman's, has worked to the advantage of the entire California wine industry. The creation of the new value-priced segment and a host of new wineries to supply it have created a lot of new consumers. In fact, hundreds of new labels have come out since 1999, many of them under $10. These labels have used up thousands upon thousands of gallons of surplus wines. Moreover, if this new value tier didn't exist, California grape growers would have been in worse shape, because grape prices would have been depressed even further.

While Two-Buck Chuck is still a viable label, it may be feeling the effects of value-priced offerings from Australia and California, which sport interesting new labels, eye-catching graphics, and vivid colors that attract younger consumers. The Australians have been particularly creative with innovative branding and packaging concepts. They even have a screw-top variety that is now sweeping the market. Overall, the Australians are set to become the largest exporter of wines to the United States, after surpassing Italy in 2004.

Can the Charles Shaw label compete with the Aussies and other value wines for market share? The answer is unclear. A lot depends on the current grape crop that, by some indications, is coming in a bit light in terms of supplies. Nonetheless, the marketplace is returning to a more stable position. There simply won't be any giveaways of super-low-priced wines, as in 2000 when Two-Buck Chuck emerged.

However, the label can still be serviced out of Franzia's own vineyards, and he may be able to maintain the $1.99 retail price.

With distribution costs remaining so low, the brand has room to take a price increase and still remain profitable for Bronco and Trader Joe's.

This has kept a lot of Two-Buck Chuck imitators from cropping up. Several food chains like Safeway went to other producers and made deals to have $1.99 wines available. However, these products are generally not featured as prominently as they are in Trader Joe's, and actual prices sometimes end up being more like three for $10. Such is the case with Sea Ridge, another low-cost wine that Franzia created for Safeway, according to Fredrikson.

The question, however, is whether a supermarket with a successful wine section really wants to put a $1.99 bottle in the middle and kill margins on the rest of the business. Trader Joe's is believed to be making about $5 per case on the Charles Shaw wine, giving it a relatively healthy profit margin of about 20 to 21 percent. If prices do go up, it will be due to cost pressures at Bronco, including higher glass prices, soaring energy costs, and the fact that Franzia is not getting the bargain grapes and surplus wines he was two years ago. In addition, while crops are hard to predict, no one is rushing to plant. Therefore, no significant surpluses are likely in the next couple of years.

"As it is, I think he's really had to push a pencil to make this work," says Fredrikson. Ironically, some of Bronco's other brands have lost ground, because so much emphasis has been put into keeping Two-Buck Chuck at $1.99. "Why buy Forestville for $1.99 or $3.99 when you can buy Charles Shaw for $1.99 and it's pretty much the same quality?" asks Fredrikson.

On the positive side, the addition of other varietals like Shiraz is bringing some new interest to the label. With some great reviews at recent wine competitions, positive press for Two-Buck Chuck has been on the rise again, and people have flocked to the stores to try out the offering. Consumer demand could jump even further if other new varietals are added to the line.

Does this mean Two-Buck Chuck will be around for the foreseeable future? "I think so. But that's only another two or three years in wine industry terms," Fredrikson offers, noting that the label's longevity may depend on whether any significant surpluses crop up to impact the market in the next couple of years.

Robert Smiley, a leading industry consultant and professor of wine industry studies at the University of California at Davis, agrees that Two-Buck Chuck is something of an oddity in the wine business brought about by the last surplus. On the other hand, its development has not been unusual. "One of my CEO friends noted that every time we have a big surplus, something comes along—like wine coolers," Smiley says. "They came in fashion and went out just as quickly. Also the idea of a drinkable $2 table wine is only new here, not in Europe."

With demand falling off a bit and the surplus worked off, Charles Shaw now has the challenge of returning to a steady, stable financing model to survive and be profitable in the long run. Fred Franzia believes he can do it. But industry observers contend that Two-Buck Chuck's future is up in the air, because the last surplus has dried up, making it virtually impossible to get comparable grapes for the same price. Maintaining the same quality means paying more for grapes, and any price increase could play havoc with retail profits. "So it's not clear there's a long-term future here—at least until the next glut cycle. And you can bet your bottom dollar that will happen again at some point. Even so, there's the question of whether consumers will tire of it," Smiley says.

However, the key to the survival of "extreme value" wines is whether consumers are willing to settle for a $2 or $3 bottle of wine that's undrinkable. Unless there's another surplus, producers simply will not be able to pay very much for the grapes that go into it. This means continually going south in the Central Valley to find affordable grapes. The problem is that the further south you go, the hotter the climate and the worse the quality of the grapes. This being the case, the $1.99 price tag for Two-Buck Chuck can be maintained. But what consumers will get is little more than grape juice in a bottle. That's fine for someone who sets out to buy a $2 wine and doesn't expect anything else. But it will also drive away consumers who were attracted by a combination of low price and high quality.

Trader Joe's is already adapting to this reality. The chain has moved the Charles Shaw label from the front to the back of the store in many locations, giving that prime space instead to newer, hipper, and more expensive brands—especially those from Australia.

Many of them are certainly more expensive, and sales among Trader Joe's customers are brisk. Still, everyone wonders, what will be the company's next Two-Buck Chuck?

CHAPTER 9

Foster a Loyal Workforce

"Hi. How are you today?" asks a smiling, Hawaiian-shirted stock clerk as I enter the store.

"Fine. Just looking around," I reply.

"Great. Let me know if you need anything. We've got some great products in," he says, bouncing down the aisle and straightening out the shelves as he goes along.

At the back of the store, a perky, raven-haired woman behind a kiosk that looks like a B-movie version of a beachfront bar in the tropics is sampling a vegetable medley.

"You've got to try this one. I sautéed it with some chicken and the kids loved it," she tells a young mother with a four-year-old squirming in the back of the cart. "You can really use anything with it. If she doesn't like it, bring it back," she adds spooning samples into little plastic cups for other customers who are starting to appear.

Twenty minutes and three more "Can I help yous?" later, I reach the register, where a teenage girl is bagging groceries for an elderly woman and her husband. "Are you going to be all right, or can I get you some help

with the cart?" she asks, as the woman shakily maneu-
vers toward the exit.

She then turns to me. "Hi. How are you today? Did
you find everything you need?"

I assure her that I did. "Aren't these great?" she asks,
scanning my bag of peanut butter–filled pretzels.

As she hands me change from my $20 bill, she actually
looks me in the eye and says sincerely, "Have a nice day!"

Exchanges like these are more the rule than the exception
at Trader Joe's, where store employees go out of their way to
engage customers in conversation and, in a nice way, tout some
of the store's new items. In many respects, this kind of attention
is the polar opposite of what consumers have come to expect
from conventional supermarkets, where turnover is high, customer service is virtually nonexistent, and employees often spend
more time complaining about their jobs than doing them.

Much has been said about the quality and value of Trader
Joe's unique array of products, the fun shopping environment
with the retro feel of a mom-and-pop store, the company's strong
relationships with suppliers, and the creativity and tenacity with
which it searches out items from around the world for one of
the industry's most distinctive and successful private label programs. Without question, all of these things are an essential part
of what makes Trader Joe's such a thriving retailer when much
larger chains are struggling to survive.

But there's a saying in retail circles that the last 100 feet are
the hardest. Every effort can be made to heighten the efficiency
of the supply chain and get products from the manufacturer to
the retailer's back door in the most cost-effective way possible.
Yet, if in-store execution is shoddy, retailers simply end up shooting themselves in the foot.

A big part of this execution—or the last 100 feet—at Trader
Joe's is its employees, people who like what they do, go out of
their way to help customers, and even engage in some sugges-

tive selling. They are a major reason for the company's success. After all, few employers—particularly in retailing—can boast of having such high levels of employee loyalty, not to mention extremely low turnover.

COMPENSATE WORKERS WELL

The core of this allegiance is a wage and benefits package that is typically far more competitive than that of most companies in the supermarket industry. Wages may attract high-quality employees, but wages are not necessarily the reason they remain loyal, as any human resources expert can attest. Employees stay because Trader Joe's has created a culture of success: an environment in which everyone does the same job at one time or another and a place where people's opinions are respected and talents are nurtured.

On first blush, this sounds a bit like the West Coast communes of the 1960s, where sharing everything from work to food drew a generation of young idealists. But at Trader Joe's, it's just good business. Indeed, the retailer, which also prides itself on the opportunities it offers everyone, from young workers putting in just a few hours a month to help pay for college to store managers, has been cited as one of the best places to work by *Fortune* magazine, joining the ranks of such estimable employers as Harley-Davidson, FedEx, Ford Motor Company, and Southwest Airlines.

In a world rocked by layoffs, cutbacks, corporate scandals, and labor unrest—particularly in retailing—Trader Joe's has long adhered to the philosophy that happy employees make for happy customers. Happy customers spend more and visit the store more frequently. This attitude is rare in the retail industry at large, where employees are often seen as expendable.

Because of this philosophy, Trader Joe's is one of a handful of companies responsible for what is seen as a paradigm shift in the retail industry, according to human resources expert Mel Kleiman of Humetrics, an internationally recognized authority on recruiting, selecting, and retaining hourly workers. "They've taken the approach that the employee is number one," Kleiman observes. "They feel that if they treat employees the way they want employees to treat customers, odds are stores will have a better shot at providing a unique shopping experience for people as soon as they walk through the door."

This objective makes Trader Joe's a tough place to land a job, which is also true of companies like Southwest Airlines, Whole Foods Market, and The Container Store, all of which only hire applicants who fit their strict customer service–oriented mold. But Trader Joe's takes it a step beyond the basic recruitment process. The company firmly believes that formal training and the product knowledge that people gain on the job results in work that's more interesting than what you'll find at your usual supermarket. Interesting work keeps employee retention levels high. It's difficult for someone to give up the fostering environment at Trader Joe's to go somewhere else.

In some ways, the employee philosophy at Trader Joe's is similar to the one espoused by Aldi, its German parent company. In an effort to control labor costs, which are among the biggest expenses on any retailer's profit and loss statement, Aldi and Trader Joe's take a somewhat bare-bones approach to the amount of labor needed in stores at any given time. However, they don't scrimp on pay.

For its management training program, Aldi makes extensive use of executive recruiters and woos applicants with a generous financial package that includes a starting salary of about 36,000 (about $47,000) annually plus pension benefits. To get the most motivated people into its 12-month training program, the company offers new hires a fully expensed company car— an Audi A4. This is an attractive perk for recent college graduates, one of the key targets of the chain's recruiting efforts.

Aldi is not one to be frivolous when it comes to labor costs at any level in the company. Luxuries and status symbols are rare, and even top executives may be required to fly coach. The cars are not available to all employees, just some of those in the management training program who are being groomed to become district managers with responsibility for six to eight stores. Because they will get a car anyway, Aldi provides them with one from the start of their training and also allows unlimited use of the vehicle for private purposes. The chain knows that, for young people starting out, the cost of having a car is sky-high, and having this expense off their backs is just as good as getting more money in their paychecks. It also fosters incredible loyalty among people who might otherwise bounce from job to job seeking a better deal.

ENCOURAGE MULTITASKING

The big difference between labor practices at Aldi and Trader Joe's seems to be operational. Both firms expect the best from their people, but Trader Joe's is a bit more informal, counting on and encouraging employees to multitask without regard to job descriptions. As such, it's not unusual for store managers to sweep the floors, stock shelves, and work the registers when the need arises. This is all part of a collaborative working environment that is valued by employees and transparent to customers. Although a collaborative or informal working environment can look somewhat haphazard to outsiders, it is an extension of Trader Joe's accelerated employee training. As the company itself has said, "The key to our continuing growth and success is our crew. We cannot grow without providing our crew with an environment that allows them the freedom to be themselves so they have the ability to be their best."

The first step in developing the right employee environment at Trader Joe's is the Leadership Development Program. This is made up of separate modules that isolate tasks and experiences needed to oversee stores and the personnel in them. The program is designed to allow people to make their own decisions about store operations, including product mix and in-store displays. This training is particularly important because employee autonomy is so highly valued.

Trader Joe's University focuses on management, leadership, and communications skills. Trainers conduct off-site university classes, each with an average of 15 to 25 students, at every stage of an employee's professional development. But store managers and assistant managers—"captains" and "first mates" in Trader Joe's parlance—are encouraged to mentor and coach "novitiates" (supervisors in training) as well as other full-time and part-time associates, referred to as the "crew." This mentoring is essential, because managers and assistant managers for the company's growing roster of stores are promoted from within, also an Aldi trait. In fact, most of them started as part-timers, an indication that the training program, combined with other adjunct efforts to take care of the workforce, is effective at attracting and retaining good people.

SCREEN WELL AND SET CLEAR RULES

Aldi, whose store managers would never think of addressing another store employee as "dude," seems a bit more intense about screening potential candidates and offering prospective employees more clearly defined roles. This philosophy, according to the chain's United Kingdom Web site, creates a "positive, frictionless working environment." Job descriptions at Aldi are short and precise and are followed faithfully by individual employees. These descriptions are also part of a sophisticated control system in the form of spot checks.[1] For those who do enter Aldi's 12-month intensive training program, the addition of the car and other benefits brings the total compensation package up to £51,500, or approximately $62,300.

Sometimes creating clearly defined roles and expectations can give rise to very strict labor policies that apply to both store employees and executives. One example is rather extreme but is a good indication of what Aldi demands. The chain has a strict no-alcohol policy for employees at work. When a former country manager of Denmark was caught drinking champagne at a store reception, he was fired instantly. "It was an innocent, business-related reception where champagne was being offered to other people," says Oliver Heins, an analyst for Planet Retail in London. "It didn't seem to make any difference that he was the one who turned that operation from being unprofitable to profitable within two years."

For both Aldi and Trader Joe's, creating this largely harmonious environment means keeping unions out. This is not too difficult given the generous wage and benefits packages. But in one landmark case, Trader Joe's won an injunction in 1998 against an organization called Progressive Campaigns in California. The organization began soliciting signatures outside a store in Santa Rosa, California, and harassing customers by blocking free access to the stores, according to Trader Joe's attorneys. The injunction established once and for all that California residents didn't have the right to free speech or assembly at a privately owned, freestanding store.

In addition to wages, Trader Joe's also offers respectable job opportunities in an industry that has, with few exceptions, rarely been considered a hot or even a viable career path. Certainly, one reason is that about 65 percent of the overall supermarket industry's workforce is made up of part-time employees. The workforce is heavily skewed to teenagers, for whom stocking shelves, slicing cold cuts, or ringing a register is hardly glamorous nor the stuff from which career paths are made.

However, if money is the prime motivator, Trader Joe's may jump-start more than its share of careers in the food industry and will most likely never be a union shop. The company pays employees an average of $21 per hour, compared with an average of $17.90 at union operations. Add to that health insurance and retirement benefits, and you've got all the ingredients of world-class labor practices that don't go unappreciated by employees or unnoticed by customers. Consider last year's four-month strike by grocery clerks in Southern California. When picket lines went up around stores operated by Kroger, Albertsons, and Safeway, customers flocked to Trader Joe's, and sales soared an estimated 30 percent.

Even first-year novitiates, or managers in training, can have a very lucrative financial package. According to the latest available figures from the company, the total compensation for first-year personnel at this level comes to $47,429. This includes an average salary of about $40,150, plus an average bonus of $950. As a sweetener, the company contributes about $6,329 to the employee's retirement fund at this salary level. Other features of the compensation package at Trader Joe's include medical, dental, and vision insurance; life and accident insurance; and paid time off. Additionally, the company conducts *quarterly* performance reviews, usually an annual affair at most chains. But what really sets the chain apart is the company-paid retirement plan under which the company contributes 15.4 percent of an employee's annual gross income to a tax-free income retirement account.

Looking at other wage rates, a first mate—an assistant store manager—pulls down an average salary of $67,930, an average bonus of $14,000, and a retirement contribution of $12,617, bringing the total compensation package to $94,547.

The captain or store manager—a position that, as noted, entails everything from management duties to sweeping up— has an average base salary of $79,455. But average bonuses based on performance come to $35,000, and a retirement contribution of more than $17,000 at that level brings the entire compensation package to more than $132,000[2]—among the highest in the entire supermarket industry.

Small wonder that when a Trader Joe's store opened in Los Altos, California, in the fall of 2003, the company received more than 500 applications for just 50 available jobs.[3]

A liberal wage and benefits package may be the optimal way to recruit people, but it doesn't necessarily get them to stay, notes Blake Frank of the University of Dallas's Graduate School of Management. "Trader Joe's is not typical of most retail establishments," Frank says. "A liberal benefits package does give them a competitive edge from a recruiting perspective. People looking for a new job look for money. But pay is not why employees generally remain with an organization."

RUN A TIGHT SHIP

Despite these liberal benefits, Trader Joe's is not about to throw around money carelessly. To control labor costs, overall store payrolls are kept down by having a lower head count in each location per dollar of sales. There are exceptions, however, according to Alex Lintner of The Boston Consulting Group. Lintner explains that at a cash-rich time like Saturday afternoon, when the store is wall-to-wall customers, as many as 18 people may be working in the back room and in the front of the store, compared to a maximum of 10 people at other times. Some industry insiders would argue that labor rates at Trader Joe's are excessive given the state of the industry and the size of its stores. However, this forward-thinking chain is buying more than just warm bodies. It pays more because its standards are higher than those of the average grocery store. Rather than seeking the disengaged worker who is simply looking to make an extra buck, so prevalent in retailing these days, Trader Joe's focuses on finding highly motivated people with a talent for customer service. A willingness to relocate is also an advantage, because the company is continually expanding into new markets and still prefers to promote from within.

Most important to the company are employees who share its values, have a passion for food, and can provide a level of customer service that makes every shopping experience fun.

Perhaps the best description of what the company looks for in its captain, novitiates, specialists, and crew comes from the company itself. "Our captains are customer satisfaction experts, ambassadors, food tasters, personnel specialists, merchandisers, problem solvers, and community volunteers, and they know their way around a luau. Upbeat, outgoing personalities blossom in this flexible environment, and a good sense of humor never hurts."

MAKE IT FUN

As one recent article on the company noted, the qualifications for employees at Trader Joe's might be more often associated with the *gentil organisateurs,* or GOs, at Club Med than a grocery clerk.[1] (In French, *gentil organisateur* translates to "congenial organizer" or "gracious/friendly host"—like social directors in charge of making sure that people staying at the facility are taken care of and have a good time.) Supermarket industry observers underscore this point time and again. "I think it's probably fun to work there because they don't take themselves too seriously," says Dan Raftery, a Chicago-based retail consultant and regular Trader Joe's shopper. "It's a very positive environment, not oppressive, stale, or negative."

Contrary to employee attitudes you run across in many conventional supermarkets, everyone at Trader Joe's, from the captain on down, truly appears to enjoy what they do. "They don't seem to feel bad about being there," notes one retail consultant, adding that he's observed the same attitude at Trader Joe's stores across the country and doubts it's a coincidence.

"You get paid well, go to work in a Hawaiian shirt, eat good food, and talk to people. This is all part of that unique culture that the chain has cultivated," says Sandy Skrovan, vice president of Retail Forward, a retail consultant based in Columbus, Ohio.

It's also part of what Neil Stern, vice president of McMillan/ Doolittle in Chicago, calls the Trader Joe's gestalt. "It's not only about product but also an attitude and lifestyle that extends to people in the store," Stern says. "This makes them [Trader Joe's workers] markedly different from employees in traditional supermarkets. It's like being part of a club. Personally, the fact I shop there means I'm educated and won't get sucked in by big brands and paying a lot of money for packaging. So I describe myself in very complimentary ways when I tell you I'm a Trader Joe's customer. It's the same thing for people who work there. It's complimentary. It's a cool place to work—fun, informal—and they sell great stuff. Frankly, the labor turmoil in the rest of the industry has worked to the advantage of Trader Joe's." Stern is alluding to a four-month retail clerks' strike in Southern California in 2004, which boosted business for Trader Joe's, along with the cloud that continues to hang over labor negotiations in other parts of the country.

"Look at places like Whole Foods, Stew Leonard's, and Wegmans," Stern continues. "It's no coincidence that great stores to shop at are also great places to work—and all of them nonunion. You can create a great marketing campaign, a billion-dollar ad campaign with glitzy flyers, but you can't fake store morale. You want to know about Kmart? Walk into a store and talk to employees. Trader Joe's is just the opposite."

YOUR PEOPLE ARE YOUR BRAND

Clearly, the chain sees its own people as a way to build brand recognition for the store. The attitude within the corporate office is that the people it hires, trains, and promotes are just as important as the low prices and products it carries.

As such, Trader Joe's is known for treating employees with a measure of respect and dignity that is virtually unequaled in the supermarket industry. Everyone from vice presidents to clerks are encouraged to come up with new ideas, all of which are taken very seriously and often acted upon. "In an environment where the hierarchy is leveled and you're appreciated for your contributions—how could you fail?" asks consultant Gretchen Gogesch, who notes that employees personally test a lot of the new products that eventually make it to the shelves. "It creates rabid employee loyalty and, in turn, genuine caring for customers."

While Trader Joe's stores have very clear spending and behavioral guidelines, they have few execution guidelines—meaning the corporate office may tell workers *what* to do but not *how* to do it. Basically, the company believes that people—given the opportunity—usually make good decisions about things like signage and merchandising.

But Trader Joe's is not just about the individual. Part of the chain's allure to prospective employees is the opportunity to be part of a collaborative working environment. Along these lines, the chain has established a peer network in which managers talk to and work with each other on developing and implementing best practices at work. "They operate six or eight 'mother' stores across the country where they try a lot of new ideas. If an idea works, they have what they call a show-and-tell visit," observes The Boston Consulting Group's Lintner. "They pick up other store managers and take them to mother stores so everyone can see what's being done."

All retail chains have certain "test stores." But, as observers point out, the trick is allowing people in the field to share information on successes and failures. "Everyone talks about teamwork and the team approach to store development," says one retail executive. "Trader Joe's has taken it from lip service to reality."

There is little, if anything, that Trader Joe's doesn't do right when it comes to recruiting and retaining what is generally considered to be one of the retail industry's best staffs. One reason is that virtually everything it does runs counter to conventional industry wisdom.

Most companies typically think that what an individual brings to an organization dictates job performance and how long they stay with an organization. Industry experts don't dispute the importance of job performance on its own. However, says Blake Frank of the University of Dallas, research shows that what an organization does for its employees once they get there has a huge impact on retention and performance. Frank learned this firsthand while coauthoring a recent report from the Coca-Cola Retailing Research Council entitled "New Ideas for Retaining Store Level Employees."

For hourly workers, there are three classes of characteristics related to employee retention: providing directions, equipment and supplies, and immediate supervision. Using either formal classroom training or on-the-job experience, Trader Joe's clearly fills the bill on all three.

Providing directions is simple, but many retailers fail in this area. It simply means that workers need to know what to do to be able to do it. "If employees don't know what to do, they become frustrated. This leads to job dissatisfaction and employee turnover. It's important that a company provide written guidance for a job, but [it must] also focus on the results and not just the task itself," says Frank, adding that Trader Joe's focus on training and the importance of simply treating customers well is one reason for its significantly lower turnover rates.

OFFER IMMEDIATE FEEDBACK

This point ties directly into the area of immediate supervision. "This is an important but broad area," says Frank. He emphasizes that it covers such areas as recognizing employees for doing a good job and how supervisors communicate the goals of the organization. For hourly workers, like those at Trader Joe's, immediate feedback from managers and assistant store managers is essential because of the high levels of customer service required. "When supervision falls down, it impacts the whole organization, and there's lots of research showing that when people leave an organization, it is because of their immediate supervisor," Frank observes.

The average retention rate in the Coca-Cola study was 97 days, meaning that 50 percent of new hires left within that time. Moreover, when half of a company's workforce is turning over every 97 days, that turnover gets expensive. In a nonunion environment like Trader Joe's, it costs approximately $2,286 to replace a cashier. When you factor in the customers who might be lost due to longer waiting time at the checkout and other factors, the cost of replacing an employee jumps to $4,200. And just because an employee is a part-timer doesn't mean he or she is inexpensive.

Frank and other observers believe that companies like Trader Joe's are doing things that make a difference. For instance, managers help out at the checkout and sweep up when needed, which workers down the chain see. Crew members also get the supervision and feedback they need, which helps to boost morale. More important, actions like this help to create good long-term employees who, like many of those who start on a part-time basis at Trader Joe's, are looking for a career path and a company that will help them to grow.

Fostering that career path, however, means leveling with prospective employees on the nature of the retail business. Trader Joe's makes it quite clear that there is a downside to being in such a fun and rewarding environment. The company states up front to potential hires that hours can be long and weekend work is common, especially for entry-level positions. But, as David Arnold, a workforce consultant with Pearson Reid London House, notes, "Some grocers are going out of their way to give people a realistic definition and expectation of the job. Telling people who walk in the door what they need to be successful in that environment helps turnover. It's when you don't tell people what they're getting into that there's a problem."

Another area in which Trader Joe's excels is in showing people what some call the "rainbow" or "light at the end of the tunnel." Demonstrating that there is a career path, or at least opportunities for advancement, helps bring higher-quality people into the organization from the outset. "It's good that [Trader Joe's has] been able to show how people move up in the organization and that it's not necessarily going to take six or seven years of scanning products to get there," Arnold says. "You have to show them they can move up in one or two years, or else you start to lose good people."

A strong upward and downward communication chain underscores the management and organizational style adopted by Trader Joe's. This means fostering a belief that the store group operates as a team and that individual opinions are valued, rather than an environment where people speak out and are either not heard or have their opinions suppressed.

Consumer activist, corporate gadfly, and sometime politician Ralph Nader has often said that large organizations today act like lords and masters and that most employees have been sufficiently desensitized to act like serfs. Whether this is true is up for debate. But employers usually get the employees they deserve. That being the case, Trader Joe's gets some of the best.

CHAPTER 10

Outsmart the Competition

It was 11:00 AM by the time the three men arrived at the Trader Joe's on Market Street, the crisp October morning warming to the touch of the autumn sun that danced on the glass windows of the surrounding office towers in Philadelphia's Center City district.

"How about a cup of coffee before we go in?" the casually dressed consultant asked, pointing in the direction of a nearby Starbucks. The two retailers, dressed in suits and ties, shook their heads and looked over at the recently converted industrial building.

"Let's go through the store first. It won't take long," said one. The other suit agreed, as they both watched more customers make their way toward the Trader Joe's entrance. The trio made their way across the street, dodging midmorning traffic and passing through a throng of office workers, area residents, and college students. Among other things, they commented on how the entrance in the back of the building, near the parking area, seemed to be ill-conceived and inconvenient.

"I want you to see this," said the consultant, picking up several copies of the *Fearless Flyer* and handing them to the two suits, who thumbed rapidly through the brochures before rolling them up. The men walked the first couple of aisles, stopping every few feet to pick a product off the shelf or out of a display case—among them a bottle of Trader Darwin multivitamins, a jar of Trader Joe's blueberry preserves, and a package of Trader Giotto's frozen eggplant parmigiana. As they walked, the consultant kept talking about the Trader Joe's private label products and the layout of the store, his monologue punctuated only by the occasional employees stopping to ask, "Are you gentlemen finding what you need?" They nodded, smiled, and started walking a bit faster, anxious to speed up the visit.

Barely 20 minutes later, they were finished. As they left, the consultant asked what they thought about the store and whether they had any questions. "No, not really," one of the suits replies. "What's next? I'd like to see some supermarkets."

Over the years, this same scene has been played out many times with retailers, wholesalers, and suppliers. Supermarket executives from across the United States and overseas, along with other potential competitors and students of retailing, have visited Trader Joe's locations from coast to coast, comparing them to each other or to their own operations or just seeing for themselves what the fuss is all about. In the end, they either learn from the experience or dismiss the stores as not a real competitive threat, often the latter. Especially dismissive are executives who were brought up in conventional supermarkets, once the most common shopping destination but now assaulted by numerous alternative formats for which food has become an essential part of operations.

"We used to take people from traditional supermarket chains through the [Trader Joe's] stores 15 years ago in Pasadena. For the most part, we got a lot of blank stares," said one consultant.

"The stores were ugly, everything was packed in boxes, and they didn't see any brands. That was probably the biggest thing bothering [the supermarket chains]. They couldn't understand why people were going there. In reality, a company like Kroger with all their resources could be in the same business tomorrow if they wanted to do it."

But most of the large supermarket chains "just don't get it." They see Trader Joe's as merely an interesting idea—an anachronism in the supermarket industry, something that really shouldn't be able to exist in this hypercompetitive universe where 60,000-square-foot stores stocked to the rafters with national brands are the rule rather than the exception. Even these are under siege by 250,000-square-foot Wal-Mart supercenters. These people only look at the store and crunch the numbers, trying to get a handle only on the bottom line and return on investment. In doing so, they often miss the point and the simple artistry that makes Trader Joe's successful. This group should also be aware that, according to the latest consumer trends report by the Food Marketing Institute in Washington, D.C., only 72 percent of shoppers now consider a traditional supermarket their primary grocery store.

Others who visit this near legendary retailer clearly do get it and ardently admire the creativity, culture, and operational simplicity that make Trader Joe's an unqualified success. On the other hand, they can't seem to get a handle on how to replicate this success within their own companies or whether they can launch a similar format that would compete on the same level.

BE YOURSELF

The bottom line is that Trader Joe's is outsmarting the competition simply by being itself. Therefore, it is an impractical model for the typical supermarket chain to adopt from either a sales or profit standpoint. When entering a market, Trader

Joe's is not so much a direct competitor to anyone as it is an addition to the marketplace. What Trader Joe's does simply doesn't fit the retail mold—at least not the one that has developed over the past several decades. The fact is that, in today's competitive climate, this is an anti-supermarket, which shouldn't even be able to survive, let alone flourish. Consider the following factors, which work so well in this esoteric brand of retailing but would be impractical for chain competitors to duplicate:

- Small stores that are generally one-sixth the size of regular supermarkets
- In-store layouts that are difficult to navigate
- Insufficient parking
- Inconvenient locations
- No national brands, eliminating the use of manufacturer coupons
- Limited variety of 2,000 to 2,500 products—10 percent of what consumers find in their typical local supermarket
- No special sales or promotions
- Emphasis on private labels, which represent 80 to 85 percent of all items stocked.

Until recently, Trader Joe's stores didn't even have scanning equipment at the checkouts, because management felt it would cut down on the interaction between customers and cashiers. When the chain finally gave in, executives spent an inordinate amount of time listening to the tone of the beeps made by various scanners to make sure the one they picked would not interfere with conversation. The fact that scanners speed up front-end operations and get consumers out the door as quickly as possible seemed to be a secondary consideration. Trader Joe's would much rather you stick around, and customers seem content taking their time to browse. Based on these factors alone, mainstream supermarkets not only couldn't compete but probably wouldn't want to try.

Convenient, highly visible locations; sale prices; bigger stores with endless selections of national brands in every conceivable size; and ever-larger perimeter departments (produce, meat, deli, and bakery) have become the trademarks of the supermarket industry. Chains have used these fundamentals to differentiate themselves from the competition. Because of this, many supermarket executives and managers feel that trying to emulate an operation like Trader Joe's would constitute a giant step backward. Unfortunately, these same elements have become an albatross around the neck of many in an industry plagued by overexpansion, a total lack of differentiation, and razor-thin profit margins.

Basically, specialty grocers succeed by concentrating on understanding and serving a specialized market, something that few of the dominant grocery chains in the country can do effectively, according to Phyllis Ezop, president of Ezop & Associates consulting and a lecturer at the University of Chicago's graduate school of business.

Dominant supermarket chains, on the other hand, have succeeded by excelling in and exploiting the mass market. They find it difficult to focus on specialized segments and, by and large, have not been effective in targeting them. They are largely preoccupied with major issues like consolidation and the competitive inroads made by chains like Wal-Mart. Trader Joe's has carved out its own niche in an industry that is heavily reliant on a mass-market mentality, not on emulating the mom-and-pop stores of yesteryear.

Even among specialty grocers, Trader Joe's is unique, embracing a combination of organic, ethnic, and health-oriented foods rather than focusing on just one of these categories. As architect and industry consultant Kevin Kelley notes: "As long as they don't try to position themselves (as a one-stop supermarket), they're doing great."

Similarly, retail industry consultant Bill Bishop says the company will not be vulnerable unless it tries to respond to competitors by growing too quickly or abandoning its current marketing and pricing strategy.

Nevertheless, there's only so much of the consumers' food dollar to go around. "The grocery business is, in effect, a zero-sum game," according to Bert Hambleton of Hambleton Resources in Seattle, Washington. The addition of Trader Joe's in a new market, "will definitely take something out of somebody else's pie."[1]

GO YOUR OWN WAY

Trader Joe's came into being in the first place because founder Joe Coulombe was looking for a way to compete against the large chains that were encroaching on his marketing area. He was a proponent of differentiation long before most supermarket executives knew what the word meant, and he did it by offering items the other chains didn't. To this day, the chain's major competitive strength lies in identifying and finding products that people want—and sometimes those they didn't know they wanted. This is done largely through an unusual array of private labels, which would be difficult for any chain to copy, along with very close relationships with suppliers. Here, private labels have become more than just an addition to the merchandise mix—they are central to its differentiation in the marketplace.

Over the years, the company's strength meant doing the polar opposite of its chain store competition. This includes refusing slotting fees from manufacturers, a practice which became so widespread among supermarket chains and wholesalers, observers have joked that the industry has made as much money taking fees from suppliers as it has from selling groceries. In the past few years, some major chains like Wal-Mart have taken a page from the philosophy espoused by Trader Joe's and gotten away from slotting and other fees, preferring instead to get the lowest prices and passing that value on to shoppers—and their own bottom line. Trader Joe's is not like Wal-Mart, which is bound and determined to be the low price leader in every category in every marketing area. Besides, having low prices that meet or beat the competition is only one of many factors customers consider.

The practice of refusing additional fees and allowances from manufacturers means more than just low prices. It means that every item on the shelf is there because that's what the customers want—not because a manufacturer is paying "rent" for the space. Listening to what customers want means that stores can take on as many as 25 new items a week—no small feat for such a small store. But as Audrey Dumper, vice president of marketing for Trader Joe's East, has said, "We like to think of Trader Joe's as an economic food democracy."[2] As such, the company has studiously avoided any sort of loyalty marketing or frequent shopper programs and doesn't collect information on customers—not even zip codes. However, its close ties with customers, who are usually quite vocal about what they like and don't like, have enabled the chain to collect the kind of information it needs to keep on top of its game—feedback that dictates which products get on the shelves and how long they stay there.

MAKE YOUR MOVES WHEN OTHERS AREN'T LOOKING

In the current competitive climate, outsmarting the competition is more important than ever. Academics and retail pundits agree this means taking them on when they are distracted by internal issues or preoccupied with outside factors. The weightiest external factor facing retailing today is Wal-Mart. Over the past several years, Wal-Mart has become the world's largest retailer and has made significant inroads into the food business through gigantic supercenters and an aggressive expansion program, giving fits to conventional supermarket operators.

But outsmarting the competition—whether Wal-Mart or any-one else—doesn't just mean keeping up with them. It's also a mat-ter of outthinking competitors and beating them to the punch.

As hockey great Wayne Gretzky once observed, the secret to success is not skating to where the puck is but rather to where it's going to be. This brings up the question of how well you know your markets, your customers, and whether you're skat-ing in the right direction.

Despite the success of such megaretailers as Wal-Mart, fo-cusing on the largest competitors may not be the right strat-egy—particularly for a retailer like Trader Joe's. Instead, sights should be set on the one or two competitors that are most vul-nerable. In an industry whose battle cry is survival of the fittest, the best way to outsmart the competition is to exploit their weaknesses—be it long checkout lines, bad employees, ineffec-tive advertising, or poor merchandising. What we are saying is that operators need to know as much about their competition and the marketplace as they do about what goes on inside their own four walls. Basically, if you don't know why customers are unhappy with your competitors, how can you offer them some-thing better? On the other hand, you can't place all your bets on the incompetence of the competition.

Efforts to outsmart the competition—whether another su-permarket, mass merchandiser, drug store, health food outlet, or wine shop—should include various strategies. Among them are the following:

- Analyze and redefine your market.
- Concentrate on specific competitors.
- Concentrate on specific markets.
- Analyze inquiries from unhappy customers or suppliers.
- Watch for competitive activity like cutbacks in advertising or loss of focus on key products.
- Spend more money when business is tough, and it will come back when times get better.

- Be ready to move on and try something different when your competitors catch on to what you're doing.[3]

These elements are part and parcel of a long-term strategy that seemed to disappear during the Internet frenzy of the 1990s. Everyone's goal—even the retail community's—was to get big fast. All that seemed to matter was size. Many companies, including those in retailing, equated long-term strategy with operational efficiency. Sometimes the two work hand in hand. But they are often mutually exclusive, and an efficient company is not necessarily the most competitive.

Perhaps the true essence of long-term strategic thinking comes from Dr. Michael Porter, author, management guru, and Harvard business school professor. "You must set limits on what you're trying to accomplish," he says. The company without a strategy is willing to try anything. If all you're trying to do is essentially the same thing as your rivals, then it's unlikely that you'll be very successful. It's incredibly arrogant for a company to believe that it can deliver the same sort of product as its rivals and actually do better for very long."[4] As such, a focus on operational efficiencies can create a mutually destructive form of competition, where everyone in the market is trying to get to the same place and consumers inevitably end up choosing their store based on price.[5]

DON'T BE ARROGANT

Trader Joe's is anything but arrogant, and it has already accomplished many, if not all, of the strategies on the aforementioned list. In fact, the company may have more in common with Wal-Mart than with other retailers. Sam Walton's success was based on his keen awareness of his company's image and his ability to meet the needs of his customers. In other words, find out what your customers really think about you and your competition. Just asking them—whether through a casual interview or formal research survey—conveys the message that you care about their needs.

Using this strategy as well, Trader Joe's has not so much outsmarted its competition as distanced itself from it, preferring to take the road less traveled. To be blunt, Trader Joe's has little, if any, direct competition. That's why its stores can operate profitably in the shadow of far larger chains. Furthermore, its stores may do better in close proximity to conventional supermarkets, because the relationship between them is more complementary than adversarial. Through this symbiosis, Trader Joe's feeds off the larger stores, which don't give customers the same experience or products. The local A&P will not carry pistachio mousse torte or light brie. Similarly, Trader Joe's will not carry Coke, Pepsi, or other promotionally driven staples.

This alone goes against conventional wisdom in an industry that, for the past 70 years, has been conditioned to believe that the only way to succeed is with national brands and national brand advertising. Trader Joe's, which has no brands and little, if any, advertising, has used its *Fearless Flyer* to develop a successful, direct, consumercentric marketing campaign.

Despite the obvious size differences previously noted, the closest "competitors" to Trader Joe's—if you really want to use that term—may be Costco warehouse stores and Whole Foods Market. Both have extensive and successful private label programs—Kirkland and 365, respectively. Private labels, or in-store brands, are clearly a key element in profitability as well as in establishing close ties to customers.

Costco's strategy is also to create an interesting shopping environment and keep treasure-hunting consumers coming back to see what's new. As at Trader Joe's, customers know that if they don't buy something at Costco when they see it, the item may not be there the next time around. On the other hand, customers at conventional supermarkets are secure in the knowledge that they will find the same products week in and week out. This works out well when it comes to product quality and a consistent selection of staples. However, consistency can easily cross the line into mind-numbing uniformity. When that happens, you run the risk of boring shoppers with plain vanilla stores that offer the same thing every week. Consistency, Ralph Waldo Emerson said, is the hobgoblin of small minds; it stifles creativity.

On the labor front, Costco is also known throughout the industry for its generous pay and benefits package, which not only keeps the union at bay but also keeps employee turnover far lower than at conventional supermarkets. As discussed in Chapter 9, the wage and benefits package offered by Trader Joe's is one of the most generous in the industry and provides a major competitive advantage in a business that continues to struggle with widespread labor unrest.

Whole Foods, like Trader Joe's, is expanding into urban markets. It focuses on a more upscale customer along with health-oriented products—most of it organic, natural, and GMO-free—not usually available at other local stores. Although Whole Foods stores are large, they also offer a feeling of intimacy—the ambiance of a neighborhood store rather than a chain. And like Trader Joe's, Whole Foods is aware that it will never be the principal supermarket for most consumers. It therefore focuses on targeting a more educated and upscale clientele who are not interested in walking the retail equivalent of a mile just to come up with a few bargains.

Trader Joe's itself has said that its principal competition is not conventional supermarkets but local health food, wine, and cheese shops.

BREAK DOWN THE SILOS

The ability of Trader Joe's to stay ahead of potential competitors also lies in the changing nature of its headquarters and executive staff. Several years ago, the company was more like its chain competition in that the corporate office tended to operate in silos. This often prevented functional areas like marketing, merchandising, and buying from interacting—a characteristic usually found at larger, more inflexible firms. Chairman and CEO Dan Bane and his senior executives recognized that this could have a negative impact on the chain's future growth and have attempted to break down those silos, making it easier for the headquarters staff to share tasks and goals.

Part of the solution, one familiar to many companies, was to consolidate offices. The company had been in South Pasadena for about 25 years and, as it grew, was forced into renting office space across the street from the original headquarters. Corporate employees, instead of being all together, were spread out over a one-block area. One of John Shields's final acts as CEO before handing the reins over to Dan Bane was to secure the current corporate headquarters in Monrovia, California. This was the beginning of a more collaborative environment, not to mention the development of an organizational structure better designed to serve the company's needs as it expanded.

The question at this point is whether further changes in the organizational structure need to be made as the company grows. Unlike some competitors who simply want to have the largest stores, biggest selection, and cheapest prices, the overarching organizational mission of Trader Joe's is to be a national chain of neighborhood stores—kind of a gourmet 7-Eleven. But how will the company maintain organizational control as it expands to 500 stores? The big question is whether it will avoid the organizational crisis that has ensnared other growth companies.

As the chain expands and sets up shop in more regions of the country, it is realistic to assume that some control—other than buying—may have to move out of its Monrovia headquarters. To a degree, this shift has already happened. The company has presidents for its Eastern and Western stores. Before taking the reins as CEO, Dan Bane had the position in the West. Key decisions still come out of Monrovia, but as the company becomes more decentralized, it may be even less vulnerable to local competition. Not having top management from a parent company constantly looking over the shoulders of executives certainly works to Trader Joe's advantage. The Albrechts gave up operational control a long time ago. Basically, Aldi representatives fly in once or twice a year, tour some stores, look at the numbers, and fly home again. Although Aldi keeps an iron grip on its other operations around the world, it is curiously hands-off when it comes to Trader Joe's, the thinking being, "If it ain't broke, don't fix it."

However, as the company grows, things like cost control—one of Aldi's specialties—become more important issues. Can entrepreneurial organizations like Trader Joe's coexist with traditional corporate thinking? Will cost control dictate standardization? Trader Joe's stands out from the competition because of its unique nature. Decentralization could be tricky, unless the people brought on board at the regional level buy into the overall corporate goal and can nurture the Trader Joe's culture at the regional and local levels.

Another question, one that may impact its ability to compete, is whether the company will continue the practice of only using cash flow to open new stores. Most industry observers do not believe that Trader Joe's will start borrowing capital to accelerate growth. For one thing, Aldi has vast resources that could be tapped. However, fiscal prudence is one of Trader Joe's major attributes. Setting reasonable limits on growth may be a good thing, because it will enable them to avoid the costly over-expansion experienced by other chains. This is the same pattern followed by Aldi and may be one of the best practices picked up from Aldi years ago. "Whatever growth they have is paced by their profitability," according to consultant Bill Bishop. "They're not little hogs at being profitable because they realize they have to propagate the culture. But my guess is that it's only recently that they have begun to grasp the true power of what they have—something that could be 15,000 stores if they wanted it to be."

Generally, the thinking is that Trader Joe's could eventually open 1,000 to 1,500 stores. One of the dangers of growth is that it will put the chain squarely on the retail radar screen. The more visible one gets in retail, the greater justification for someone to come along and copy what you're doing. Additionally, the larger a company gets, the harder it is to maintain a niche strategy. But this is a smart, conservative company in a niche that holds tremendous opportunities. Also, working in Trader Joe's favor is that it does not occupy a single niche that can be replicated by competitors. It operates on the fringe of several niches—including health foods, wine, discount foods, and gourmet products—offering enough of each to tantalize shoppers and keep them coming back but not enough to make a significant impact on any one category. It simply does everything in moderation and creates its own unique niche or culture.

The central strength of Trader Joe's will never be about opening massive numbers of stores and saturating the market to gain share. It stays above the competitive fray by finding, identifying, and rolling out new items—not the product proliferation so prevalent in the supermarket industry at large but unique offerings. These items fit the store's image and appeal to a discriminating customer base that doesn't shop Trader Joe's for mass-market items.

Meanwhile, minimizing the number of unique stock-keeping units (SKUs) enables Trader Joe's to reduce the capital investment required to support the stores, also giving them a competitive edge. This means that with stores making $100,000 per week in sales—and many do far more than that—the chain is, as one observer noted, "making a ton of money."

Clearly, cost control is key. Minimal number of items and high inventory turnover are critical strategic initiatives that Trader Joe's has maintained. And even though it only carries some 2,000 to 2,500 items per store, the chain is constantly culling items that don't work and introducing new ones. Conventional stores can't compete with that kind of flexibility, and they don't even come close to its cost structure because of the relatively few, nonunion employees working at each Trader Joe's store.

The issue is not so much how other stores can compete on this level as whether they really want to at all. For its part, Trader Joe's is completely comfortable being across the street from large anchor supermarkets. It's as if they are a small fish riding on the back of a whale in a kind of peaceful coexistence.

At times, the feeling is mutual. Some chains have learned to live with Trader Joe's, accepting the fact that this specialty store will pick off a certain percentage of their sales. They know that a conventional format simply can't compete. Large stores can't create the same kind of easy-to-shop, informal atmosphere. This is not to say they're not interested in the concept. "In the past several years, everyone has been looking at Trader Joe's," according to Kevin Kelley. "All of a sudden, Wall Street bankers are asking about them. The shopping center industry is looking at them, and department stores want to know more about them. *Funk* and *quirky* are 'in.' I'm really surprised that no one has tried to imitate the concept. That's what they do in the restaurant industry when something is successful. Everyone copies it."

Kelley further notes that the industry's preoccupation with Wal-Mart, Costco, and other big-box formats—even dollar stores—has left Trader Joe's in the background, where it likes to be, while the competition focuses its attention elsewhere. "They [the big chains] notice when a 99-cent store moves in across the street. They even worried about chicken sales when Boston Market was big," Kelly observes. "But they're not worried about the Trader Joe's concept the way they should be. Only in the past couple of years have they even acknowledged that Trader Joe's is a potential threat."

The chain is what Ken Harris of Cannondale Associates calls "an obtuse competitor," meaning that it doesn't fit squarely into anyone's competitive set. Aside from a hard-core fan group, no one really does all their weekly shopping at Trader Joe's. They take consumers away from traditional channels in increments, chipping away little by little at sales in certain categories. But the company has been able to insulate itself by not really competing head-on with anyone. As noted, the products that Trader Joe's sells will not be found in local supermarkets.

Mainstream supermarkets find themselves in the middle, being marginalized by chains at two ends of the spectrum— Trader Joe's nibbling away on one end and companies like Whole Foods picking off sales on the other. Mainstream supermarkets do not so much ignore Trader Joe's as just don't know what to do with it. "They would know what to do if Trader Joe's was a direct competitor like Aldi or a limited assortment supermarket like Big Lots," Harris says. "You go after them on the basis of price and selection of national brands. But how do you go after something like Two-Buck Chuck? You can't, unless you want to get involved developing your own $2 bottle of wine. Basically, they've come up with some impossible propositions for competitors to deal with and assembled them all in one place."

However, competitors are certainly not helpless. Any number of them could pick off a handful of things that Trader Joe's does well—including high-quality private label items, organic products, and ethnic foods. The issue is how to pick off enough of them to get people to switch their shopping behavior. That's not to say Trader Joe's is invulnerable. Some observers believe that its Achilles' heel may be its limited selection, and any competitor who comes up with a similar format with greater breadth and depth of selection may be able to take a bite out of the chain's growing sales.

REACH FOR THE TIPPING POINT

Five years from now is when Trader Joe's will probably pop up on the competitive radar screen the way Aldi and Starbucks have done. "Starbucks started in 1973 but didn't hit anyone's radar screen until the 1990s," notes Harris. "All of a sudden they were an 'overnight sensation,' which had taken 25 years to build. It's going to be the same way for Trader Joe's."

What it will take is what author Malcolm Gladwell has termed *the tipping point*—a moment at which change happens quickly and unexpectedly and all of a sudden everyone takes notice. Trader Joe's has yet to reach the tipping point but will get closer as the company continues its current store opening strategy and expands into major media centers like New York with a high concentration of stores. "Starbucks's tipping point was when they reached eight of the ten major media markets," Harris explains. "It might be just the same for Trader Joe's."

As the chain moves into new and unfamiliar markets, gathering more consumer data may become a more important competitive issue than it is now. Of course, a big part of its success has always been the interaction that takes place between customers, employees, and store managers. This interaction is yet another way for the company to gauge its image in the marketplace. Because competitors ostensibly do the same thing, more formal polling of existing and potential customers might have to be done through quick and simple telephone surveys, mailings, Web sites, or company newsletters.

A succinct, easy-to-complete survey conducted on a regular basis could turn up some interesting marketing and merchandising issues rather than waiting for them to come up in casual conversation with customers. Following up with people will reinforce a positive impression and will help guarantee they'll come back, and getting people to return is essential for Trader Joe's. After all, visiting the store is not an absolute necessity for most consumers when it comes to their weekly shopping. However, even mainstream supermarkets are wrestling with frequency of visits these days. Additionally, in such a hotly competitive climate, surveys might turn up interesting insights on why some consumers no longer shop at the store, or shop there less frequently, and what would entice them to return.

At the same time, these surveys should also be used to turn up information about competitors and what can be done to surpass them on such measures as customer service, product quality, or price. It may also reveal data on market niches that have yet to be explored by Trader Joe's or any other retailer, while indicating that it may be time to adjust or change one's image. However, a change of image could be a tricky move for Trader Joe's, because the current one is so imprinted on people's minds that even a slight change could alienate longtime customers. The other concern is that a company revamping its image could be seen as being forced to change due to competitive pressures. Neither scenario is acceptable, but neither of them is completely unavoidable.

Basically, consumer market surveys can be boiled down to ten basic questions.

1. What is the nicest thing about doing business with us?
2. What were the deciding factors in choosing our store?
3. Are there other products and services we should offer?
4. How can products and services be improved to meet your needs?
5. Rate our organization on the following factors—value, stability, commitment, quality, flexibility, responsiveness, and innovation.
6. Rate our competitors' ability to deliver the products and services you expect.
7. How do our prices compare with those of our competitors?
8. What frustrations have you encountered when dealing with our company?
9. How can we attract more customers?
10. What can we do to keep you as a valued customer?

The key is to use marketing information not so much to change a strategy or image but to refine it on an ongoing basis. Even for Trader Joe's, whose image is that of David to the chain stores' Goliath, change is inevitable. As with everything else in business, you just have to make sure that whatever you do isn't too little, too late. There is scant chance of this happening to Trader Joe's, especially because its smaller size makes it more flexible and able to react more quickly to changes in the market than its larger counterparts can.

Sam Walton's philosophy was to know his competition intimately, copy their best ideas, and always be on the lookout for things that can be done better. For Wal-Mart, conventional supermarkets, airlines, and even department stores, truer words were never spoken.

CHAPTER 11

Don't Be Boastful

Last year, the *Mail Tribune* in Oregon's Rogue Valley area conducted an online survey among shoppers, asking which retailer they'd most like to see come into the area. Editors were surprised by the record response. Even more startling to some was that Trader Joe's was at the top of the list. The chain received more than four times the number of responses garnered by second-place finisher Nordstrom's.

In 1995, a group of "PTA moms" in San Carlos, California, began an intense letter-writing campaign, sending thousands of postcards to Trader Joe's headquarters, asking them to consider opening a store in this Northern California community. After much cajoling and a little wheeling and dealing, work finally began on the site in 2004, and people are continually asking local politicians when the store will open.[1] In Chicago's Lincoln Park, people lined up for hours waiting for a Trader Joe's grand opening. The same scene was repeated in Cambridge, Massachusetts; Bellevue, Washington; Santa Fe, New Mexico; Reno, Nevada; and numerous other towns and cities across the country. There are even stories about people coming from as far as Saudi

Arabia to stuff a couple of suitcases with items from Trader Joe's that are virtually impossible to get anywhere else at any price.

But not everyone is familiar with Trader Joe's. After all, word of mouth doesn't always travel quickly, and people need time to figure out what this unique company is really all about. One woman in Missouri actually walked into a Trader Joe's thinking it was a furniture store. But she seemed to catch on quickly and walked out with several bags of groceries, not at all disappointed by the lack of tables and couches. Indeed, generally little or no advertising or promotional activity heralds the arrival of a new Trader Joe's. Whether to announce the opening of another location or to increase traffic at existing stores, the company believes that word of mouth is the best form of advertising and that public relations is best left to the public.

SPEND AD MONEY SMARTLY

For years, advertising has been the lifeblood of the supermarket industry. Television, radio, newspaper, and circular ads are constantly clogging consumers' consciousness, bombarding them with sales pitches. Frankly, the industry's tactics haven't changed all that much over the past five decades. If anything, the advertising in a growing variety of venues has become even more important to all retailers. For one thing, promotional money from manufacturers is often tied to the amount of space an item gets in the ads and the frequency with which that item appears. The bottom line is that ad money has become a key profit center for many retailers, one they are loathe to give up.

Additionally, and perhaps most important, the retail arena has become increasingly crowded with everyone from drug chains and discounters to office supply and department stores selling food. Under these circumstances, the amount of money spent on advertising—as inefficient as that spending might be—has increased exponentially. A look at the Sunday circulars, or even the multipage ad inserts dropped in daily newspapers during the week, provides clear evidence that advertising is as important as ever—at least to mainstream retailers.

By this time, you've no doubt grown to understand that Trader Joe's has always been an oddity within the supermarket industry at large—a maverick that seems to avoid anything even remotely conventional. This is no less the case when it comes to advertising and attracting media attention. This company historically has only opened 15 to 20 stores a year in various parts of the country. Any normal company would, at the very least, pump some heavy local ad spending into the budget or start wooing the local media in advance of an opening to generate some buzz. However, the advertising strategy at Trader Joe's is simply to do some local radio spots—which sound more or as like they did in the 1970s—and selectively to mail out its promotional newsletter, the *Fearless Flyer*.

The latter is a bit like preaching to the choir, because most of those who get the *Fearless Flyer* are already Trader Joe's customers. Many of those who aren't have at least requested it, so they are not totally unfamiliar with the stores. Even if they're not customers now, they're likely to be very soon. This strategy is the essence of simplicity in a world that sometimes seemed ruled by over-the-top advertising. The chain has never viewed extensive and expensive advertising as an effective way to brand the store and doesn't believe in using it merely as a way to be seen. That's why you'll never see flashy television ads with a screaming spokesperson extolling the store's virtues.

Frankly, the company doesn't need to resort to such conventional—and often ineffective—marketing means, because its average consumer is not trying to decide whether to go to a Trader Joe's or a conventional supermarket. That decision has already been made. Besides, no other store has the products that shopper is looking for. The chain is a perfect example of what can be done in the area of marketing and public relations without spending millions of dollars on ad campaigns that do nothing but promote commodities. It is about building a brand and an image that deliver on the promise of high-quality foods in a comfortable environment, served by people who make consumers feel good about their purchases. It's not about saturation ad campaigns, banging the drum as loudly as possible, or burning your logo into every inch of a consumer's consciousness in an effort to take business away from the competition. This is a perfect example of that often talked about but little-used strategy—*less is more.*

What seems most important to Trader Joe's is to generate goodwill among its legion of loyal customers. Goodwill is not some intangible and mysterious line on a corporate balance sheet. For Trader Joe's, it means everything from letting people sample items before they buy, giving them a full refund if they don't like a product, offering good prices, and encouraging lighthearted communication with employees who are the front line of the chain's low-key public relations strategy.

SHUN THE LIMELIGHT

Strangely, the chain sometimes seems more intent on shunning the limelight than breaking into it. Because neither Trader Joe's nor Aldi are public companies, there is little, if any, benefit in talking to the business press—especially with regard to sharing any of their business secrets. After all, why tip your mitt to the competition or become grist for the rumor mill? As such, most journalists' requests for interviews with top executives are met with a predictably polite but terse thanks-but-no-thanks response. The one-sentence e-mail response this author received to an interview request from chairman Dan Bane was more than the European press gets from executives at the parent company. Aldi is notoriously closemouthed with the business and consumer press in Europe, whose requests for interviews or even innocent comments are often met with stony silence.

Then again, the chain's spokesperson, while cordial to the consumer media when it comes to store openings in new markets, generally offers little more than trite sound bites and basic information. This company values its customers but also treasures its privacy and is willing to bet the farm that shoppers really don't care if executives cooperate with *Business Week, The New York Times,* ABC News, or the *San Jose Mercury News.*

Although the chain continues to make limited radio buys in some markets, the bulk of its "media" strategy revolves around three things: word of mouth by loyal shoppers who offer unsolicited testimonials on products to complete strangers, loquacious employees, and the *Fearless Flyer.* This folksy brochure, printed only five times a year, is more popular today than when first introduced by founder Joe Coulombe in the 1970s.

Of course, this strategy could all be a big ruse according to some observers, who believe the chain's reticence to talk is somewhat calculated. They surmise that it adds to the Trader Joe's mystique among consumers who have yet to discover this niche retailer, while making regular shoppers feel as though they are part of an exclusive club. No one gets the sense of being part of a family by reading the weekly supermarket circulars. But mention the *Fearless Flyer,* and those in the know will extol its virtues as if they were bragging about their own child.

The *Fearless Flyer* is particularly well suited to Trader Joe's, a company more intent on communicating with customers than advertising or marketing to them. In fact, many customers refer to the chain's communications as "messages" rather than advertising. It's as if they are talking to a friend who is treating them with respect—not a faceless corporate entity.

Trader Joe's is pretty much the polar opposite of every other food chain, for whom weekly circulars, newspaper ads, promotional allowances from manufacturers, and press releases are a way of life and a nasty habit to break. Trader Joe's strategy also runs counter to the recent trend of embracing technology for in-store advertising, such as television screens in the aisles or at the checkout or wireless devices on the back of shopping carts that track a consumer's movements through the store, reminding them of product specials as they walk along. This approach is definitely not the Trader Joe's style.

"Basically, the strategies you see in the supermarket industry lack excitement. There are a lot of items and prices, but nothing's really creating a point of differentiation," says Richard George, author and professor of food marketing at St. Joseph's University in Philadelphia. "I always challenge people to look at the full-page ads or circulars from four major competitors with the tops cut off and tell me who each belongs to. A lot of money is being spent on not a lot of differentiation."

Put another way, much is being spent by the retail food industry on advertising and publicity in the name of brand awareness. But is this merely throwing good money after bad, a case of spending simply to be seen without really giving consumers a reason to shop at your store?

When things go awry, the problem is usually a broken connection between retailers and their customers. Branding is not about throwing ill-conceived advertising into the marketplace to gain awareness and build some kind of image. It's about refocusing on relationships with customers.[2] As Pat St. John, vice president of marketing and chief spokesperson for Trader Joe's, has noted, "We keep our promise. No amount of advertising can create what we want to create with our customers. Advertising can remind people, but it can't create an experience. It's the personal relationship with these people that builds loyalty."

CREATE A SENSE OF COMMUNITY

The history books are loaded with examples of entrepreneurially minded people who knew the value of connecting with customers. Josiah Wedgwood did it with pottery in the 18th century when he positioned upscale products to attract Britons of lower economic status. More recently, cosmetics diva Estée Lauder constantly changed the company's product line as she talked to customers to find out what they wanted. And Howard Schultz of Starbucks didn't just create a demand for latte. He and the company created a sense of community in a disconnected world.[3] This sense of community, in turn, creates an emotional bond with consumers and develops a subculture that requires few, if any, advertising reminders. It is highly reminiscent of everything that Trader Joe's has done since its inception.

On a dollar-and-cents level, advertising is still a big business for the nation's mainstream supermarkets. During the most recent reported period, food retailers spent a median of 1 percent of sales on advertising, according to the "2004 Food Marketing Industry Speaks," a comprehensive look at the supermarket industry published annually by the Food Marketing Institute (FMI) in Washington, D.C. This figure was pretty much the same as reported the previous year. These expenditures probably would have been higher had it not been for a sluggish overall economy and extensive across-the-board cost-cutting measures.

A breakdown of ad spending for the industry at large clearly shows the differences between Trader Joe's and its contemporaries. Overall, newspaper ads accounted for the largest percentage of expenditures—56.7 percent. It is interesting to note that newspaper advertising accounted for nearly 76 percent of the ad budget among food retailers with less than $10 million in annual sales. Presumably, smaller chains and independents feel that newspaper ads are a better vehicle to reach a local constituency. But the question remains whether they speak to the needs of the people who see them. Apparently they do, according to FMI's report, which also noted that more shoppers were scanning newspapers for grocery specials. However, the value of advertising also depends on which shoppers you're trying to reach. Younger shoppers are less likely to check newspaper ads for grocery specials, while women use them far more often than men do.

After newspaper ads, direct mail was the biggest ad expenditure for grocers, accounting for 10.8 percent of retail budgets. Independents outspent chains in this medium simply because direct mail reaches a more targeted market. Radio, a medium that Trader Joe's occasionally favors, accounted for 7.3 percent of retail ad budgets during the most recent period. One of the smallest pieces of the ad budget, and coincidentally the closest to Trader Joe's strategy, is targeted mailers. Target mail accounts for only 3.8 percent of the ad budget, yet it may be the most effective way of reaching a specific customer base.

Meanwhile, marketers of every stripe are beginning to delve into the effectiveness of advertising expenditures across the board. For example Procter & Gamble, whose brands are among the biggest global advertisers, is involved in a new system called Project Apollo. Project Apollo seeks to quantify the results of advertising by collecting data on which media consumers use for which products.[4] This study will enable the company to calculate a return on its advertising investment—something that Trader Joe's really doesn't have to do because its expenditures are relatively minuscule. But it does speak to the need for more effective and targeted advertising, something Trader Joe's has already accomplished.

A little different picture of supermarket advertising emerges when you look at it from a consumer's perspective. Here, ad inserts—circulars that are often indistinguishable from one another—are used by 56 percent of women to decide where to shop for groceries. Additionally, 87 percent of principal grocery shoppers use them to compare prices, and 69 percent of all people use circulars to plan their shopping trips based on advertised items, according to a study by Vertis, a market research firm based in Baltimore, Maryland. Of course, this doesn't mean that a company like Trader Joe's should start doing inserts. The people surveyed may shop at Trader Joe's. But it's not where they go for their primary weekly shopping trip. And if they do go to a Trader Joe's, it's for different reasons and different products.

Trader Joe's has been able to capitalize on customer desires by selling not just products but also a unique shopping experience. "They are one of a handful of companies out there that are not turning their backs on the consumer. They don't look at their shelves like chain buyers. They try to see what the consumer sees," says George.

This kind of publicity spreads by word of mouth among consumers. Shoppers create this publicity for the chain. As more people come to the stores, they tell their friends, and the chain gets more than its share of free advertising. Then, when Trader Joe's comes to town or is even scouting locations for new stores, it's an event.

Of course, the unusual lineup of private label items is a huge draw for customers. It's a big part of the low-key image imparted by Trader Joe's and is key to its awareness-building campaign. But part of the chain's strategy has been to develop a reputation among consumers as the place to go for information. Inside the front entrance, part of one wall is set aside for information sheets and brochures with detailed information on everything from soy and organic products to the calorie, fiber, and fat content of virtually every item in the store. Other sheets may discuss which items are kosher, which are either low-sodium or sodium-free, or those that are gluten-free. This informational "advertising" is as important to Trader Joe's shoppers as the weekly price insert put out by conventional supermarkets.

"We did a focus group recently where we asked people where they got information on new, value-added dairy products," George observes. "Most of them said they went to Trader Joe's."

This theme of being the go-to guys for information on a variety of topics is brilliantly carried through by the *Fearless Flyer,* which both serves to bolster the chain's low-price but gourmet image and offers entertaining, tongue-in-cheek stories about its unique products. The circular also tells where the items came from and why you'll be better off for having bought them— whether it's black peppered cashews from southern Thailand or Moroccan tangine simmer sauce. These aren't the kind of items or promotions you'll see advertised by the local Safeway or Kroger. "A recent holiday edition was 28 pages long. It was designed to make people better shoppers and homemakers while helping to keep the company's advertising costs down—savings that are passed along to customers," George says. For Trader Joe's, the answer is just not to do a lot of advertising.

The *Fearless Flyer* has further become the vehicle for Trader Joe's to add a little "romance" to the store and to the overall shopping experience. "I like to stand outside of retail stores and ask people why they shop there. When you ask about supermarkets, the usual response is 'It's close to home.' When you ask the same question outside a Trader Joe's, they say, 'It's fun and people talk to you.'" This is part of the company's very subtle public relations campaign, which is all produced in-house rather than by expensive public relations and advertising agencies, whose services would be of questionable value. "The story Trader Joe's creates for itself has real allure for shoppers and creates a value perception," George adds. "They are not really low price, but they do a great job of creating that image. The best advertising for them has been word of mouth among customers."

GROW THE MESSAGE

Will Trader Joe's be able to use this same low-key approach as it moves along a more aggressive growth path? Setting economic circumstances aside for the moment, chain retailers typically boost ad spending as they grow to capitalize on more cost-effective ad buys and to promote a single, cohesive message across a broader area to more consumers. On the other hand, eschewing traditional advertising altogether is not unheard of. The best example of this is Starbucks, and Trader Joe's may follow in its footsteps. Starbucks spends very little on advertising, preferring instead to throw the bulk of capital into locations and facilities. That green-and-white logo has become instantly recognizable and has spread a subculture across the country.

Oddly enough, Trader Joe's and Wal-Mart are very much alike when it comes to advertising and promotional strategies. Wal-Mart may be into television advertising in a big way, but it looks neither for slotting fees nor for ad allowances from manufacturers, both of which have, as noted earlier, become profit centers for many retailers.

Still, will Trader Joe's eventually have to rethink its advertising and public relations strategies? Consider the basic function of advertising. Above all else, it is a vehicle for building awareness. To what extent does Trader Joe's need to build awareness when entering new markets? Chains that spend tons of money on advertising are usually old-line retailers whose offerings people already know. Often, this advertising does nothing more than reach customers who are already coming to the store week after week.

A more traditional and frequent advertising program could help the chain build some awareness in new marketing areas, notes Todd Hale, senior vice president of ACNielsen. "But once they get located and people hear about them, they get the traffic they need anyway," Hale says. For the most part, a change in ad and promotional strategies would only be considered if another competitor with similar offerings moved into their marketing area—a highly unlikely scenario given the unique Trader Joe's image.

However, as the saying goes, never say never. Whole Foods, the major player in the organic and health-oriented retail arena, was rolling merrily along on minimal advertising until its competitor, Wild Oats, got into the feature and price game. Whole Foods found that image alone can't sustain the balance sheet, and the chain is hurting according to some sources.

Trader Joe's, like Starbucks, prefers to put the bulk of its money into the shopping experience and into getting people who only shop at the stores sporadically to come back more often. The company would rather promote the actual shopping experience than buy ads comparing itself to conventional retailers.

MAKE THE WEB EXCITING

If there is a place where Trader Joe's falls a bit flat in self-promotion, it may be on the company's Web site, which is far less exciting than it should be, according to some observers. However, it does present a fairly complete picture of a company that doesn't take itself too seriously and is anything but frivolous with corporate funds. It may not be pretty in the eyes of a Web designer, but it accomplishes what Trader Joe's is best at—telling a story. The easily navigable site answers what is usually the most important question first: what the company is all about and what it stands for. It accomplishes this through a brief mission statement and history, punctuated by the same Victorian era clip art used in the *Fearless Flyer* that looks like something out of a 1960s Monty Python sketch.

The site also offers an explanation of the *Fearless Flyer* and an opportunity to sign up online for what the company itself describes as a cross between *Consumer Reports* and *Mad* magazine. The site also has a sample of the latest issue and, for Internet savvy customers, this is every bit as effective as anything Trader Joe's could do in a regular print ad. The site also contains on-line versions of the same information sheets on products and categories found in its stores. Where the site falls short is that it does not encourage people to get in touch with the company via e-mail. It lists a post office box and street address for the Eastern, Midwestern, and West Coast headquarters, as well as a toll-free number where consumers can get the address of their nearest Trader Joe's store. However, as far as customer feedback is concerned, the company urges consumers to visit their nearest Trader Joe's location to speak with staff or store managers—

a strategy that enhances the personal contact that the chain encourages between shoppers and staff.

GO BEYOND CONVENTION

Could conventional supermarkets take a page from the chain's low-key but highly effective ad strategy? "Yes, but it would take a significant leap of faith," according to George at St. Joseph's. "The key is for some of the big guys to step up and see a better way to go to market." However, this scenario is unlikely, given that many retailers rely on the huge amounts of ad money available from national brand manufacturers and slotting fees for shelf placements. "It sometimes seems as though some retailers only want their customers to clear the shelves so they can make more money on the next buy," George adds. This is about as far away from *consumer focused* as you can get.

To be fair, the format and extensive private label offerings allow Trader Joe's to advertise differently. If you don't stock national brands, you don't have to worry about getting national brand ad money or about adjusting your advertising and promotional strategies to suit other people's agendas. Additionally, typical Trader Joe's customers are not the same as supercenter shoppers who are using weekly ads to plan their shopping trips.

Nonetheless, it's generally agreed that the major players need to wake up to the fact that the retail world has changed in terms of attracting customers with effective ad campaigns. The most vulnerable may be some of the biggest names in the business: Albertsons, Winn-Dixie (in bankruptcy at this writing), Kroger, and Safeway. Wal-Mart and Aldi have the price side covered. Companies like Trader Joe's and regional retailers like Wegmans go for the in-store ambiance. "The ones in the middle, those between low price and great service, are the ones who will be squeezed," says George.

Whether in the supermarket business or anywhere else, advertising is an increasingly complex business that is constantly changing due to shifting consumer demand and the development of new venues. For years, direct mail—a strategy quietly but expertly used by Trader Joe's—has been favored by large and small businesses alike. The problem is that traditional advertising is often measured in costs per thousand. This can be an expensive proposition depending on the audience you're trying to reach. With direct mail, pricing is cost per response; the greater the response, the lower the cost. This is not easy to calculate in an operation like Trader Joe's, especially because its entire approach to advertising is so atypical in the retail industry. Although products and prices are key parts of the company's direct-mail pieces, they seem to be more of a low-key continuing public relations tool, going out to customers who, for the most part, are already avid shoppers. As such, there's no way for the company to determine a response rate on its direct-mail pieces. At other companies, a response rate would be used to adjust merchandise selection and prices. However, Trader Joe's appears to view direct mail as enabling the company to stay close to its customers and communicate with them in an informal, fun way.

Studies have shown that people will devote a maximum of 15 seconds to direct-mail pieces, and usually far less, before tossing them. However, the average Trader Joe's customer seems to read these pieces from cover to cover, often using them as meal-planning guides instead of focusing on one or two low-priced items. This is the opposite of recent trends in advertising and underscores the type of customer that Trader Joe's attracts.

British consumer psychologist David Lewis has pointed out that ad copy is getting shorter because people suffer from acute shortages of time and attention. Younger generations are extremely visually literate, because they have been brought up on computer games, and couldn't deal with a lot of polished copy if they wanted to. While this group does not represent the prime audience for Trader Joe's, some of the same rules apply. Despite some flowery language and a bit of whimsy in telling the story of its products, the company is fairly adept at keeping things quick, simple, and to the point in its advertising, newsletters, and direct-mail pieces.

GIVE BACK

In the supermarket industry, as in others, being a good corporate citizen is the equivalent of free publicity. Chains and independent operators spend untold millions of dollars each year on extensive donation programs. Trader Joe's takes more of a grassroots approach by leaving donations in the hands of individual stores. But it also has very specific guidelines for evaluating donation requests and for what it will and won't do in the name of keeping spending down and prices low.

Sponsoring various kinds of events is common within the supermarket industry, with companies spending millions of dollars and thousands of worker-hours to keep their names favorably in the news and in front of consumers. However, Trader Joe's makes it crystal clear that it does not buy advertising, program space, or tickets to events under any circumstances. It also does not underwrite any organization—a favorite form of advertising and self-promotion by other companies—or donate gift certificates.

The company is not trying to play the Grinch. Instead, it is simply being practical and holding down unnecessary costs. Each store handles its own donations, and no organization can receive more than one corporate donation a year. The only donations are to the arts and to educational and medical causes. Additionally, the company restricts its donations to registered nonprofit groups and requires written proof of that status before writing out a check. As far as can be determined, the company, unlike other retailers, is not involved with any lobbying groups designed to influence local legislation or regulations. If Trader Joe's wants something done, it prefers to do it itself rather than through a third party.

However, the chain has no qualms about aligning itself with certain organizations and causes when the situation arises. In 2001, after a yearlong campaign by Greenpeace and other groups, like the GE-Free Market Coalition and the Genetic Engineering Action Network, Trader Joe's stopped using genetically engineered ingredients in its private label products. Some felt the chain was simply bowing to pressure by special interests to avoid what could have been a very public, image-damaging argument. Still, the chain managed to turn this move into a public relations coup by putting a positive spin on it and noting that 90 to 95 percent of customers wanted them to stop using genetically engineered ingredients.

In 2003, Trader Joe's became the darling of left-leaning animal rights groups when it became one of the first companies to receive the Proggy Award from People for the Ethical Treatment of Animals (PETA). Along with 30 other organizations, Trader Joe's was featured on PETA's Web site and got a nice plaque.

In 2004, Trader Joe's picked up kudos from the Rainforest Action Network (RAN) for its decision to stop buying bags from Weyerhaeuser, which the group cited as the "number one destroyer of old-growth forests in North America." Again Trader Joe's said it was taking action based on the wishes of its customers and its own principles. But, in this case, the chain even chastised RAN for putting out what Trader Joe's claimed was misleading information on Weyerhaeuser's products.

However, observers generally note that Trader Joe's does not get involved in organizations and causes solely as a public relations tool to sell more products, nor does it take up certain causes to pander to special-interest groups. Likewise, the company doesn't seem interested in what the competition is doing or in standing out. The chain's efforts are not about promoting itself as a destination. This company's main objective is generally perceived as simply doing the right thing.

Nevertheless, there's nothing wrong with viewing a little corporate altruism as a strong business strategy. Consumers are not stupid. They are perfectly willing to accept that companies like Trader Joe's and others want to benefit from the work they do and the vast resources at their disposal—whether corporate donations or supporting a cause.

The question is what a company's true goals are when it decides to support a cause—whether it's eliminating genetically engineered ingredients in their products or just participating in community-based programs. An increasing number of companies seem to be combining philanthropy with strategic business goals, according to a study done by Cone, Inc., a Boston-based strategy firm, and Roper Starch Worldwide, a New York–based consulting and market research firm. Asked about business objectives for cause-related efforts, 90 percent cited enhancement of brand recognition.

More than 80 percent of respondents in this study also mentioned strengthening community support, boosting employee loyalty, being a preferred employer, and developing trust with consumers. Clearly, all of these attributes are evident at Trader Joe's.

This report and others note that consumers are more likely to reward good corporate citizens and that, if price and quality are equal, consumers will likely switch to a brand or retailer that supports a good cause. Additionally, more than 80 percent of consumers in this study said they are likely to have a more positive image of a company that supports a cause they care about. One finding that hearkens back directly to the Trader Joe's brand of customer is that consumers value companies that support social issues and prefer those that are not shy about marketing their efforts. In other words, the public wants companies to be more transparent in communicating their social initiatives, according to the study.

Because many of Trader Joe's customers are inclined toward health-oriented, organic, and preservative-free types of products, a study by the Organic Consumers Association on the relationship between corporate citizenship and a company's reputation seems particularly pertinent. As in the Roper results, it was noted that more people than ever look at corporate citizenship and its impact on the community it serves when forming opinions about a chain's reputation.

Among the findings are:

- 78 percent say companies have a responsibility to support social issues.
- 92 percent have a more positive image of companies that support social causes.
- 89 percent say that, in light of Enron and WorldCom, it's more important than ever for companies to be socially responsible.

Asked what they would do if a company fails to live up to corporate citizenship standards, people responded as follows:

- 91 percent would consider switching to another company's products or services.
- 85 percent will speak out against that company among family and friends.
- 83 percent would refuse to invest in that firm's stock.
- 76 percent would consider boycotting the company's products or services.
- 87 percent are more likely to remember a company when they see information about its social causes.

Although Trader Joe's is not associated with a "signature" cause, consumers do like to see this: building values into the corporate culture. From that perspective, no one does it better than Trader Joe's.

Epilogue

There's an old saying in business that "If it ain't broke, don't fix it." This philosophy is repeated time and again in boardrooms and executive suites and at industry conferences every day across the country. It's also become the mantra at some of the nation's top business schools that, for many years, produced bumper crops of MBAs who specialized in making an impressive show of fixing things that should have been left alone.

Trader Joe's has really taken this advice to heart.

From reading this book, you've no doubt concluded that Trader Joe's is a living, breathing example of this axiom in action—a company that has avoided unnecessary fixes and profited handsomely from simply sticking to what it believes is the right thing for its customers. Don't misunderstand: This is not a company that believes in the status quo. It is a textbook example of a corporation that is quietly evolving in terms of sales, profits, and customer service—while at the same time retaining its unique character. The chain continues to build strong, long-term relationships with vendors in the United States and overseas, a strategy that has yielded a steady flow of distinctive products. This strategy is a far cry from that of the bulk of the supermarket industry, whose main preoccupation seems to be squeezing every last penny from vendors on commodity items.

The natural question is: where does Trader Joe's go from here?

Part of the answer can be found by looking at where the supermarket industry is today. The entire retail food business is in a state of flux. It is being bombarded from all sides by competition that includes drug chains, dollar stores, warehouse clubs, supermarkets, mass marketers, and even the corner bodegas. All sell food, and most sell the exact same items. Many of these outlets, which didn't even exist a decade ago, are now nipping at the heels of traditional supermarkets, stealing away sales of goods that were once—excuse the phrase—the industry's bread and butter. The pressure to sell merchandise at the lowest price— and still produce a profit—has never been greater or more problematic.

In this environment, the temptation to "fix" a store or company also has never been greater. Most retailers—food and otherwise—seem to be caught in a scenario in which change is not just an option; it's essential for survival. As such, retailers have rushed headlong into a variety of strategic and tactical directions, often adopting every piece of new technology and merchandising strategy that comes along. Or they pay enormous sums to consultants, store designers, and other experts, ostensibly to learn more about customers and what they want to buy.

Too many companies have been seduced into thinking that, the more complex the solution, the better its odds for success. This is rarely the case in retailing. For most, these "solutions" are simply an exercise in spending money—a way to pile up data without ever really knowing what it means, how to use it, or how to determine its impact on your business.

Clearly, the solution is not to change simply for the sake of change, or even to keep up with what the competition is doing, but rather to use change as a catalyst for evolving into something better—something more useful and efficient for customers.

Trader Joe's is so distinct from others in the food industry that it has no compelling reason to change. It is a niche retailer with virtually no competition. Little, if anything, is broken. As a result, there's no need for management to attempt quick fixes for problems that don't exist.

As previously noted, don't take this to mean that Trader Joe's is standing still. Like its parent company, Aldi, this chain is not given to frivolous capital outlays. Even store expansion is financed internally, giving Trader Joe's one of the cleanest, most debt-free balance sheets in the business. In many ways, this company is far more progressive than its contemporaries. It has the capacity to change but is unwilling to do so on a massive scale for no good reason. How's that for simple logic?

The format that Trader Joe's developed almost four decades ago has remained pretty much intact to this day. With some adjustments, it could probably serve the company well for many years to come. Despite the continued expansion of retail behemoths like Wal-Mart, small-store retailing has been staging a comeback in recent years. Time-strapped, shopping-weary consumers are tired of walking down miles and miles of aisles just to see the same old, same old. Trader Joe's has been, and will continue to be, a viable alternative. Its shopper base will expand exponentially as the chain rolls out new stores across the country.

However, expansion will be slow and steady. Plans calling for relatively modest growth are unlikely to change. The company's strict policy of no external borrowing, using only cash flow to finance new stores, smacks of a fiscal conservatism practically unheard of in retailing. Yet this policy may be the most financially prudent in an industry that has overexpanded for more than a decade. Taking this a step further, Trader Joe's may have one of the healthiest balance sheets in the supermarket business, a fact that has not escaped the notice of some on Wall Street, even though Trader Joe's is unlikely ever to be publicly traded. Aldi likes its privacy, and going public would require releasing too much competitively sensitive information.

Where Trader Joe's will expand in the future is as telling a discussion as how many stores it plans to open. As we have said, one of the most interesting developments is the company's move to urban markets, such as the imminent opening in New York City, where the chain's quirky style and high-quality, low-price private label products are likely to be a huge hit with Big Apple consumers.

Many industry observers believe the inner city will be a new retail battleground, the final frontier for the supermarket industry. Trader Joe's, while not leading the charge, is certainly following close behind. There's little doubt that the chain is scouting urban areas from coast to coast. Existing stores are already yielding sales per square foot amounting to more than twice the industry average. But this figure could increase even further with a meaningful move to the inner city. Given the population density of urban markets and the scarcity of gourmet foods at low prices, Trader Joe's is likely to win instant fans, even among the most jaded city dwellers.

At the same time, the company will continue to expand its presence in traditional suburban locales. Look for a trend toward somewhat larger stores. Indications are that the chain now prefers a 12,000- to 13,000-square-foot footprint rather than the average 10,000-square-foot unit of just a few years ago.

Will Trader Joe's ever try to open a 50,000-square-foot supermarket to compete with the likes of Whole Foods? Unlikely. It would be a classic example of trying to fix something that isn't broken—or trying to fix it until it is broken. Besides, Trader Joe's loyal and highly vocal customer following would probably be up in arms over the loss of a smaller, more shopable format.

Nonetheless, the chain is expanding its horizons when it comes to the types of sites it will consider. In the past, inexpensive secondary sites, primarily in underdeveloped strip centers, were its targets. These are still on its real estate hit list, and consumers don't seem to mind making the trek to these somewhat inconvenient locations to shop at Trader Joe's. However, alternatives are being explored. Trader Joe's already has stores on the periphery of large new shopping centers that include a supermarket anchor. This is a good way to build traffic without losing business to a direct competitor. In essence, Trader Joe's enjoys symbiotic relationships with conventional supermarkets, secure in the knowledge that people shop differently in its stores than at regular supermarkets. As such, there's no reason the two can't live side by side. Customers don't come to Trader Joe's for Coke, Pepsi, or five-pound packages of ground chuck. Some claim they can do their entire weekly shopping trip at Trader Joe's. But for most consumers, a visit to this store is a special event, a treasure hunt that lets people explore and get the satisfaction of finding products they can't find anywhere else. This experience differentiates Trader Joe's from the rest of the industry, and the formula likely will help it grow in the future. In fact, the only danger for the company would be if it somehow ceased to be different.

Being different also means avoiding national brands, continually changing its selection of private label items, holding down inventory and costs by dealing directly with manufacturers, and keeping selection to a relatively slim 2,000 to 2,500 items—the majority of which are Trader Joe's store brands.

The latter has elicited some debate. Should Trader Joe's move toward 100 percent private label, or should it cut back in favor of more regional brands? It appears that the chain is exactly where it should be in terms of its product mix. Anything less would be cheating customers of a unique experience. And, because private label is where retailers can make the most money, the company would only be shooting itself in the foot.

On the other hand, as the chain expands, some question whether it will move more towards mainstream merchandising to attract a broader cross section of customers. In all likelihood, the answer is a resounding no.

Moving to middle ground on merchandising would lose more customers than it would attract. A Trader Joe's with Coke, Tide, or Bounty paper towels would simply be another supermarket. That's not what the consuming public wants or needs. It is certainly not what the target customers of Trader Joe's have come to expect. If anything, trends seem to indicate that the chain will be entertaining more shoppers than ever in the future. Despite economic ups and downs, people are generally traveling more—or at least are more inclined to do so. Despite, or perhaps because of, media hype over increasing obesity in America, many are becoming more health-conscious. These folks are inclined to read labels and appreciate a good value when they see it. All of these trends bode well for Trader Joe's and are yet further reasons why this chain could conceivably become a retail powerhouse on a national—maybe someday global—scale.

We are entering an era in which brand names are often upstaged by the retailers who stock them and where the store itself has become the brand. Many department stores and supermarket chains that once represented the tastes of the American consumer are falling by the wayside, with declining sales putting increased pressure on profit margins. The same old, same old is rapidly becoming a cliché, destined to only be a footnote in the history of American business.

Retailing has never been easy. Catering to the ever-changing tastes of the American consumer will always be a constant challenge. But when all is said and done, the most dangerous ground to be on in retail is the middle ground—where you're neither one thing nor another. Rest assured, Trader Joe's will never find itself in this place.

Granted, chains like Wal-Mart and Target, along with the full-line supermarket chains that strive to be all things to all people, are still powerful entities. But we're witnessing a subtle return to the "mom-and-pop stores" of yesterday—a niche where retailers build themselves into the brand and carry things that others can't or won't. This same trend is happening in many other businesses as well. And it's at the very heart of what Trader Joe's is all about.

Acknowledgments

T hey say that "retail is detail," and no one knows the details like the people who were gracious enough to share their valuable time and insights for this project. I would like to thank Ken Harris of Cannondale Associates; Gretchen Gogesch of Integrale, Inc.; Jon Fredrikson of Gomberg, Fredrikson & Associates; Blake Frank at the University of Dallas; author and consultant Dieter Brandes for his insights into both Aldi and Trader Joe's; Pascal Kuipers of Elsevier Food International for putting up with grumpy authors; Robert Smiley at the University of California at Davis; Bill Bishop of Bishop Consulting; Todd Hale of ACNielsen; Alex Lintner of The Boston Consulting Group; Neil Stern of McMillan/Doolittle; Kevin Kelley of Shook Kelley; Richard George at St. Joseph's University; Kirk Kazanjian of Literary Productions for his guidance; Mark Mallinger at Pepperdine University; Letty Workman at Utah Valley State University; Faruk Ozdemir of Reis, Inc.; Scott Muldavin of The Muldavin Company; Phyllis Ezop of Ezop & Associates; and to a dozen other people (you know who you are) who prefer anonymity.

A special thanks to my wife and partner, Pat, for her unwavering support, good humor, and undying patience with me and my quirky personality and habits. And to my son, Jonathan, for his sage advice on this project when he said, "Stop whining like a little kid and just do it."

Notes

Chapter 1

1. Candace Talmadge, "Tapping the Urban Core," *Shopping Centers Today,* 1 August 1999.

Chapter 2

1. Euromonitor International, Chicago, Illinois.

2. Retail Monitor International, March 2002.

3. Retail Monitor International, March 2002.

4. NAMNEWS, online newsletter, http://www.kamcity.com. (See note 11.)

5. Retail Monitor International, March 2002.

6. "The Next Wal-Mart?" *Business Week* (European Edition), 26 April 2004.

7. Ibid.

8. Euromonitor.

9. Retail Monitor International.

10. M+M Planet Retail. (See note 12.)

11. NAMNEWS, Professional Assignments Group, Australia.

12. "Aldi in the USA," Planet Retail, June 2004.

13. Euromonitor.

Chapter 3

1. Tom Belden, "Unique Sales Approach at Unlikely Philadelphia Site," *Philadelphia Inquirer,* 6 September 2003.

2. Amy Wu, "A Specialty Food Store with a Discount Attitude," *New York Times,* 27 July 2003.

3. Frank Green, "On the Cheap," *San Diego Union-Tribune,* 21 September 2003.

4. Dieter Brandes, *Bare Essentials: The Aldi Way to Retail Success* (London: Cyan/Campus Books).

5. Ibid.

Chapter 4

1. "Trader Joe's Targets 'Educated Buyer,'" *Seattle Post-Intelligencer,* 30 August 2003.

2. John Boudreau, "Funky Formula: Gourmet Food at Low Prices," *San Jose Mercury News,* 13 January 2004.

3. Wine Notes, *Modesto Bee,* 23 April 2004.

4. "Trader Joe's: The Trendy American Cousin," *Business Week Online* (http://www.businessweek.com), 26 April 2004.

Chapter 5

1. Amy Wu, "A Specialty Food Store with a Discount Attitude," NYTimes.com (http://www.nytimes.com), 27 April 2004.

2. Frank Green, "On the Cheap," *San Diego Union-Tribune,* 21 September 2003.

3. "Trader Joe's Targets Educated Buyer," *Seattle Post-Intelligencer* (Associated Press story), 30 August 2003.

4. Providence Cicero, "Quirky Trader Joe's Draws Shoppers for Deals on Fine Foods, Wines," *Seattle Times*, 5 May 2004.

5. Ibid.

6. Http://www.lovemarks.com.

7. Anthony Biano, "The Vanishing Mass Market," *Business Week*, 12 July 2004.

Chapter 6

1. Robert J. Frank, Elizabeth A. Hihas, Laxman Narasimhan, and Stacey Rauch, "Competing in a Value-Driven World," *North American Retail Practice* (McKinsey & Company, February 2003).

2. Willard Bishop, "The Store Is the New Marketing Platform: Emerging Trends in Retail Marketing," *Wine Business Monthly*, March 2003.

3. Ibid.

4. Karl Albrecht, *Delivering Customer Value* (University Park, Illinois: Productivity Press, 1995).

Chapter 7

1. Maura K. Ammenheuser, "The Unsupermarket," *Shopping Centers Today*, December 2003.

2. Beth Mattson-Teig, "Convenience or Low Prices?" Retailtrafficmagazine.com (http://www.retailtrafficmagazine.com), 1 July 2003.

Chapter 8

1. *20/20*, ABC-TX, January 20, 2004, http://abcnews.go.com.

2. Http://www.winejoe.com.

3. "Two-Buck Chuck Wine Cult," http://www.cbsnews.com, 2 June 2003.

4. Tim Moran, "Wine Notes," *Modesto Bee,* 23 April 2003.

5. Mike Steinberger, "Wine for Tightwads," *Slate* (on http://www.msn.com), 22 July 2003.

Chapter 9

1. Dieter Brandes, *Bare Essentials: The Aldi Way to Retail Success* (Frankfurt, Germany: Campus Verlag, 2003).

2. Trader Joe's Web site, http://www.traderjoes.com.

3. John Boudreau, "Funky Formula: Gourmet Food at Low Prices," *San Jose Mercury News,* 13 January 2004.

Chapter 10

1. Bob Quick, "Groceries Brace for Trader Joe's," *Santa Fe New Mexican,* 16 August 2004.

2. Jena McGregor, "Leading Listener: Trader Joe's," *Fast Company,* October 2004.

3. Michael T. Brandt, "Outsmarting the Competition," *Inc.,* September 1998.

4. Keith H. Hammonds, "Michael Porter's Big Ideas," *Fast Company,* March 2001.

5. Ibid.

Chapter 11

1. Michele Leung, "Trader Joe's Closer to SC opening," *San Francisco Examiner,* 27 November 2003.

2. Curtis Pentilla, "Brand Awareness," *Entrepreneur,* September 2001.

3. Ibid.

4. Gary Silverman, "P&G Recruits for New System," *Financial Times,* 6 December 2004.

Index

ABOUT THE AUTHOR

Len Lewis has covered the global retail industry for more than 30 years. He is the former editor in chief of *Progressive Grocer* magazine and is currently a contributing feature writer and columnist for several business publications in the United States and Europe. Through his planning and development firm, Lewis Communications, Inc., he also researches and consults on projects for retailers and consumer products companies. Lewis has been a speaker and moderator at numerous supermarket industry events over the years and is a recognized expert on this ever-changing business. An avid Trader Joe's fan, he lives in Floral Park, New York.

Share the message!

Bulk discounts
Discounts start at only 10 copies and range from 30% to 55% off retail price based on quantity.

Custom publishing
Private label a cover with your organization's name and logo. Or, tailor information to your needs with a custom pamphlet that highlights specific chapters.

Ancillaries
Workshop outlines, videos, and other products are available on select titles.

Dynamic speakers
Engaging authors are available to share their expertise and insight at your event.

Call Dearborn Trade Special Sales at 1-800-621-9621, ext. 4444, or e-mail trade@dearborn.com.

Dearborn™
Trade Publishing
A **Kaplan Professional** Company